# The Blog of Maisy Malone

## by Eve Ainsworth

The Blog of Maisy Malone

ISBN 978-1-291-18955-1

This book is dedicated to Kev.

# The Blog of Maisy Malone

## About Me

My name is Maisy Malone. I'm seventeen years old, live in a ratty council house with my 60 year old, near-alcoholic Dad and a dog with a leaky bum.

I'm not really sure who'll read this blog. Jess said she *might* have a peek on her lunch break at work. Her laptop is broken. The silly cow spilt Coke on it and then tried to clean it with Mr Muscle. Now it's sparkling clean, but hisses when you try and turn it on. Sorry Jess, but that was a bloody daft thing to do…

As for Poppy, I'm never sure if she'll have much time between swooning over her Vampire films and writing her 'definite' next bestseller.

I don't care who reads this really. I guess it's nice to think that there is something of me out there in cyberspace, forever hovering in eternity long after I'm dead. Not that I'm planning on dying or anything. Even so, I was told by a toothless old crone in town that I would be dead within a month, but that was only because Billy Martin spat on her open-toed sandal and I laughed. I know I shouldn't have, but I always do when it's wrong to. Anyway, who wants to buy manky old heather? It's so naff.

I'm safe anyway, that happened in May. *I think…*

I like music, hair bands (I seem to collect them) and have an unhealthy addiction to chewing gum, even though it gives me wind.

I'm not at school, so I need a job. Or a rich man. Or a record contract. Considering I live on an estate and can't sing to save my life, the first option is probably my only one.

This is my blog. You can either like it, or you can…well… blog off!! ;o)


## Friday 22nd July 2011

### Return of the Twat!

So he's back. The twat is back.

I was woken up this morning by a loud banging at our front door. My first thought was that Dad had locked himself out again, but I quickly realised this wasn't the case.

Dad had actually gone to bed before me last night, grumbling that he didn't have enough money to pay for a pint.

The knocking terrified Dave, who was sleeping at the end of my bed. He would make a bloody useless guard dog, as he promptly leapt under the wardrobe and remained there with just his tail sticking out, like a great big hairy sausage.

The fact is, not many people knock at our front door. We have a side entrance that friends and family use and we all know the key is under the rotten, old wellie boot by the back door (Dad does tend to forget this when he's had one too many).

Someone was at the front door, and there were only three possibilities

  a)  Nanna. Nope, it was far too early for her (she's a right lazy cow)
  b)  The postman. Nah. He never shows up before twelve…
  c)  Debt collectors.

Fearing 'option c', I crept downstairs wondering if we could pretend we weren't in, or had emigrated, or were dead.

There was a large shadow looming by the glass, which didn't help identify who the caller was, so I sat on the bottom step and wondered if they would go away if I just kept quiet long enough. The problem was, if they kept banging, they were bound to wake up Dad - and the stupid old sod would open the door in a hurry to hurl abuse, not stopping to consider who might be on the other side.

Suddenly the letterbox flapped open and a pair of eyes peered through. I nearly jumped out of my skin.

A loud voice screamed.

"For Christ's sake, will one of you lazy buggers let me in?"

My heart dropped. It wasn't a debt collector. It was worse.

I got up from the step and opened the door slowly.

"Hello Maz," he said.

I couldn't quite take in what I was seeing. He just seemed to be a mess of bruises and cuts. His usually smug face was swollen and twisted slightly to one side and his right eye was a mass of red swelling.

He was standing there clutching a bright orange Sainsbury's carrier bag in one hand and his phone in the other. His blonde hair was a complete mess, all the curls falling about his forehead. He needed a shave. This was unlike my brother. Usually, he

6

looked perfectly turned out, even when he had just woken up.

My brother, back home again. Great! We actually call him the 'arsehole' in this house. And, like most arseholes, he's best left hidden.

He pushed past me and went straight into the living room.

"I tried the side door, but it was locked." He told me, like I didn't know.

*Everyone except Ollie, because of course he hasn't been home for four years.*

Meanwhile, Dave had decided it was safe to come back downstairs and was looking at Ollie with suspicion. He would only just remember him. He sniffed his leg and then, obviously not liking what he'd found, whimpered pathetically and scampered off again under the table.

"He looks like he needs a good wash," Ollie said.

"He's not the only one," I snapped back.

Ollie pulled a face at me, the 'yeah very funny' face that he always does when he doesn't like something.

I asked him what he was doing here, getting more frustrated at him. I didn't want him back home. All he does is cause trouble and upset people. It really was the last thing I needed.

He didn't answer at first. Instead, he just looked me up and down in a slow, nasty way. It was then I became conscious of the fact that I was standing there in a tatty pink nightie, and that my hair was stuck up on end. I must have looked a right state.

I stared back at him. He was a fine one to look me up and down, in the mess he was in. Strangely, he was still wearing a suit, but it was majorly crumpled. He looked as though he'd been sleeping on someone's sofa last night. He didn't smell too nice either.

"I'll be staying for a bit," he said. "Things weren't working out. I need to reassess my situation, try out some new ideas I've got. I just need a base, that's all."

But what could I say, it wasn't my house.

I asked him where Lottie was. The last time he called (about eight months ago) he kept bragging about her. She's meant to be super-important in media circles, but of course we never had the privilege of meeting her.

"We needed a break." He said simply. "It's complicated."

I didn't push it further, I didn't need to. I know Ollie too well. My brother has left a trail of broken hearts behind him, and he really couldn't care less. The chances were he slept with her sister/best friend/mother/boss (delete as applicable), because, believe me, he has done it all before. That probably explains the state of his face.

I bet you anything that he's been sacked from his job too.

I watched as he slumped down in the sofa with the dodgy springs. I prayed for one to pop up and poke him in the bum, but it didn't happen (damn!).

Reluctantly, I made him tea, resisting the urge not to put something nasty in it. Then, I screamed up to Dad, "Get your bum out of bed."

Dad came downstairs dressed in his usual attire, looking more bedraggled than usual, scratching his belly and looking at Ollie with a mixture of distrust and shock.

"Hello son. What are you doing here? Screwed up again, have you?" He was squinting carefully at Ollie's bruises. "Jesus, what the hell have you done to your face?"

Ollie muttered something about tripping down some stairs. *Yeah, right.*

Dad didn't seem to care whether that was the truth or not, he just punched Ollie's shoulder and declared 'it was great to have him home.'

This house is rapidly filling with testosterone, I'm already feeling overwhelmed. I can see myself confined to my room even more, talking to Dave like a demented mental patient.

So instead of talking to a dog (and a pretty stupid one at that), I've decided to start this blog. This will be my little bit of space, my area to write and rant.

If I'm honest, keeping this blog is also something to keep me away from my family – as I may end up killing one of them soon. Very soon, in fact…

### Comments

**JesseBelle:** Hello!! You've done it! Well done mate, your very own blog. And guess what! I fixed the laptop (well, Steve did) so I will be on here loads, pestering u!

Love the name!! Sounds like a film star.

I hope you've calmed down about Ollie now. Text me later. I wanna meet him. XXXX

**MaisyM:** Thanks for commenting babe.

He's doing my head in already. I only have to look at him and I want to SCREAM.

Will text you later x


## Sunday 24th July 2011

### Ollie

So it seems that Ollie has definitely moved into the spare bedroom. His Sainsbury's carrier bag is now empty and stuffed under the bed. It only contained some pants, a pair of jeans, a couple of t-shirts and a copy of GQ. I can't believe he doesn't have a toothbrush. I had to give him an old one that I found rammed behind the sink. I had to blow off the dust and give it a quick rinse first.

He's also brought back a small, pink teddy. I found it stuffed under the bed. (Yeah I know I shouldn't have looked but I couldn't help myself.) The bear has a little t-shirt with "lover boy" written on it. It's dead naff. I'm actually surprised Ollie has something like that. It must be *hers.*

I haven't seen much of my brother today apart from that. He's been in his room a lot and he's been out a lot more. And when I have seen him, he's been on his phone, mainly shouting.

"Lottie, listen to me!"

Or

"Look, I just need you to call me!"

Or

"I want my stuff, you silly cow! Answer your phone!"

I mean, I'm no mind reader, but something tells me Lottie doesn't want to talk to him.

I can't help wondering what he's done this time. It has to be something bad. The difference is, this time he actually looks upset about it.

## Comments

**JesseBelle:** Talk to him! Is he really so bad? I gotta meet him now...

And you shouldn't poke around in his stuff babe, that's just not cool x

**MaisyM:** Trust me, you don't want to meet him.

But I won't do it again – promise xo(


## Monday 25ᵗʰ July 2011

### Life!

You know, it's the little things that are slowly driving me mad. Like the fact that Dad remains in his underpants until well past midday. I wouldn't mind so much, only they are not even his best ones. I tried buying him some nice smart boxers from Marks last Christmas, but these have stayed in the packet, in his bottom drawer, alongside broken lighters, empty inhalers and old Viz comics.

It's not like I can bring people home with him looking like that, can I? He's like the freak in the corner.

He boil-washes his pants on the hob to try and remove the stubborn stains. I have to try and cook our Spaghetti Bolognaise alongside his rancid, bubbling y-fronts, wondering if the foul stench of his simmering smalls will affect the tomato sauce. I'm sure Nanna wouldn't approve, but she hardly comes round anymore.

My Dad just isn't normal, full stop. He probably never has been, but the last three years (since Mum slipped out of the back door and into the arms of the biker with the long nose, who has long been replaced by another biker, Sweaty Keith) have made him even more mental. At least he once held down a job. There was a time when he actually did a days' work before slinking down to the Pride for a swift half, or ten.

Now he's in the pub so much he has his own bar stool, and that is as wonky as he is. They even named the bloody pub cat after him. Poor old Clive - looks just as miserable, is just as lazy and also tends to scratch his arse a lot - although, generally, he smells better...

If Dad's not in the pub, he's slowly stagnating in his grubby armchair, watching all manner of crap on daytime TV. It's no wonder his brain is slowly melting before my very eyes.

And as for Ollie – urgh! Words can't describe how I feel about him. I hate having him back here, skulking around. It makes me feel uneasy somehow. I just know that there is a reason why Ollie is back. He wouldn't just show up, after all this time, if something bad hadn't happened. But he won't tell me. When I asked him this morning 'how long he was back' – he told me to 'keep my beak out of it'.

That's nice! And he knows I hate my nose.

I guess it doesn't help that I'm home all day now I've left school. I did my GSCEs (as I promised my Mum I would) and then I got the hell out of there. It's not like I hate learning, some of the stuff was okay. I just hated the place – the sight, the smell and, worst of all, Melissa Henderson.

So, for me, this blog is an escape. Maybe one day I will read this back and wonder how the hell I coped.

Hopefully writing this will help to keep me sane.


## Comments

**JesseBelle:** You need to get on some forums, so more people find out about this mad family of yours. Become famous, that will piss that stig Melissa right off.

Don't let Ollie upset u, maybe he's just pissed with his girlfriend or something.

P.S I saw Melissa outside my shop today. She looks sooooo rough

xx

**MaisyM:** Thanks J. Yeah, think I will try Twitter, though a bit scared as never tweeted in my life. Except when I try to talk to my Dad's stupid bird...

Ollie has been out most of the day, barely seen him (what a shame.) Mum called and I had to tell her he's home. She couldn't talk for about five minutes, she just kept doing that stupid shrieking noise she does, like when she saw Robbie Williams in town that time.

I hope you gave Melissa one of your best evils...

**JesseBelle:** Of course I did. Lol xx

**Wednesday 27th July 2011**

**Birthday Boy**

Today is Dad's birthday. The mad old sod has actually made it to 61. Thanks to Dave leaving him "another present," he nearly didn't make that. I swear his heart won't be able to take much more shouting. He's hardly the fittest of blokes.

But I was pleased because I managed to get him a present this year (thanks to Jess's Mum giving me some cash for dying her hair).

I got him a nice pair of slippers.

Not just any old slippers either. These were special ones. Ones that you could warm in the microwave and would therefore keep your toes warm on a very cold night. The website assured me it was like having your feet up in front of an open fire.

'That sounds nice,' as I thought about my Dad's withered old toes. 'He'd love my gift. He'd think I was so kind.'

I was wrong.

"These are bloody stupid!" he said in what could only be described as disgust, holding up one floppy and very stripy slipper in his hand. "They look like clown shoes. And they have no backs."

To demonstrate his frustration, my helpful father tried them on and attempted to walk across the room. It was nothing short of a demented shuffle, he looked like a ninety year old man with piles.

"I can't bloody walk in these!" he spat. "I look like an imbecile."

He went back to the box and examined it carefully with his new horn-rimmed glasses. He doesn't like his new glasses either; says he can't 'see out of them' but is persevering with them because he 'can't be bothered to go back to the Opticians and complain.'

He's so lazy…

"Ah-Ha!" He jabbed his finger at the printed instructions. "It even says here, these slippers are NOT for walking in. What does that mean then? That I have to just sit on my arse all day then?"

"No difference there then," I said back.

Norm, Dad's drinking buddy was also there, snickering in the corner like a naughty school boy. I don't like Norm much. He reminds me of Captain Birdseye, complete with fishy odour.

There was no sign of Ollie, of course. He had gone out first thing without a word to my Dad. I bet he's forgotten it's his birthday. I'm not sure whether he remembered last year either. He's such an idiot.

"But what if I want to walk? If I want to walk to the toilet and back, I'll have to shuffle there – like this…" Dad was continuing to grumble.

He did the weird penguin walk again. It was funny. I only wished I had a video camera. I could've sent it in to You've Been Framed and made a bit.

He went back to the box and continued to read aloud.

"So to heat these bloody things, I have to remove the insoles with OVEN GLOVES and then place in the microwave and STAND WELL BACK. What the hell is going to happen? Will the whole thing explode? Next I have to place the insoles back into the slippers STILL WEARING MY OVEN GLOVES (like that will be an easy job). And it says here, if the slippers are too hot – please remove immediately…."

My Dad thumped on the box.

"No, of course I won't. I will just continue to fry my feet because I'm too thick to remove them! Are these slippers for complete morons?"

We then had a burst of hysterical laughter as he finally read out; "Do not use on the very old, infirm or those that are asleep." He threw the box down. "Why would you put red hot slippers on a sleeping person? This is taking the mick!"

I asked Norm if he had done any better with his present.

"Of course I did," he replied smugly. "I got him six cans of Tennents."

Honestly, I don't know why I bothered wasting my money on him. It's not as if I'm rolling in it. I should have just brought the talc they had on special offer down the Co-op.

I've spent this evening looking for jobs on the internet, but everyone seems to want

13

experience and that's something I'm lacking. I've not yet found an advert for a "young, pretty hopeless person" experienced in "clearing up beer cans and dog poo and cooking potato waffles."

I hate being stuck at home. I thought it would be okay, but actually I'm beginning to feel a bit sick about it. I feel like I need to be doing something.

Dad's moaning because the child benefit has stopped now I'm no longer at school – the money used to go towards his tab at the Pride.

"I'd try and find myself something if it wasn't the shooting pain in my back..." he grumbles.

Pain in his back? I can think of a pain somewhere else more fitting.

## Comments

**JesseBelle:** Happy B'day Clive! Did he have a good day in the end? Where r the slippers?

**MaisyM:** Not sure. I really think he has thrown them in the bin...

**JesseBelle:** Dig them out and flog them on Ebay. My mum says you should flog the dog too while you're at it. x

**MaisyM:** I would, but no-one would want him. I think I'm the only one that loves him...

**JesseBelle:** You're a soppy cow ;o)

## Thursday 28th July 2011

### Bangers and Cash

Today I met with Mum, the woman that left us for the "guy with the long nose," later to be replaced by Sweaty Keith. My Mum seems to be attracted to complete idiots.

I was hoping that she would lend me some money, as things are getting pretty desperate. I had to pick the mould off my toast before I could eat it this morning.

The conversation with Mum went something like this:

14

*"Maisy, I don't have any money at the moment. Things are very tight."*

*"Tell that lazy arse to spend some pennies down the Co-Op instead of drowning it down the pub."*

And...

*"Do you think I'm made of money? My gigs aren't paying much you know. Anyway, Keith has debts of his own you know."*

We were sat in the dark café beneath my Mum's flat. My Mum was lounging in the plastic chair, picking at the varnish on her long, fuchsia pink, plastic nails. She wasn't eating, she rarely did – instead, a mug of tea sat in front of her strong enough to hold the teaspoon upright. She looks like a tribute to an eighties' Madonna that has gone hideously wrong, her bleached blonde hair spiked up in messy peaks and her make-up glaring in luminous tones.

Mum thinks she is nineteen and a singer. The reality is she is fifty, unemployed and occasionally sings in a dodgy tribute band. Her boyfriend, 'Sweaty Keith,' is the drummer. The sweat usually drips down his drumsticks and stains his tight t-shirts.

I picked at the congealed sausages in front of me, wondering if this would be the only meal of the day. I knew I had a can of tuna at home, so I could use that to keep Dad going.

"I just need a bit, Mum," I continued to insist. "We have no food left."

I hated begging but seriously, what other option did I have? I wasn't getting benefits (yet) and Dad had spent his in a second.

I wanted to say, "If you hadn't walked out, Mum, if you hadn't run off with that biker with the long nose, maybe Dad wouldn't have gone crazy. Maybe he wouldn't have thumped that guy at work. And maybe, just maybe, we would still have some money."

But I didn't. I just chewed my tasteless sausage and stared into her dark blue eyes; her eyes that were suddenly looking very old and very tired (although I obviously didn't tell her that!). The worst thing you could say to my Mum was that she was getting old, or ugly. Or, God forbid, both.

"Don't give me that beseeching look of yours, Maisy-Moo," she whined.

I hate it when she calls me 'Moo.' She knows that.

Mum always had high hopes for me; she even took a Saturday job in a Bookies just to pay for my tap dancing lessons when I was a kid. This was until it became abundantly clear that I was an actual danger to the other children. Ms Brewer, my moon-faced teacher, had to take me to one side at the age of seven (shortly after I had tripped and knocked three smaller children off the stage) to kindly inform me that dancing was not my forte. At that age I didn't even know what "forte" was so I ended up thinking she was saying "fault" in a funny way.

I found out shortly after that singing was not "my fault" either (apparently I'm tone deaf) nor acting (I'm a bit 'wooden'....). Therefore, mother's dreams of her only daughter hitting the West End Stage soon disappeared as quickly as a fart in the breeze.

And I think she hates me a little bit for it.

I keep reminding her that Ollie is the success of the family. Hunky Ollie, with his flashy mobile phone and tailored suits.

Mum is so excited that he is back, she can hardly contain herself. She has tried to text him. But he has ignored her so far.

"Tell Ollie that he must come for Sunday dinner, with you of course!" She told me firmly. "We have a lot of catching up to do."

"He won't want to come." I told her, trying to ignore the disappointed look in her eyes.

I'm going to accidently-on-purpose forget to tell him.

Does that make me a bad daughter? But the thought of a whole day with Mum, Sweaty Keith AND Ollie makes my skin crawl.

"I'm so excited he's back," she said, beaming. "I have a feeling this time things will be different. We can make things work."

"He won't have changed, Mum," I told her.

"You're too young to be so cynical. Of course he can change. We all can."

We didn't talk much more after that. Mum watched me eat my sausage and mash, with a faint expression of disgust in her eyes. I don't know what she was expecting; she brought me to this Greasy Spoon and I was starving. It's not my fault she lives on salads and vitamins like her stupid friends.

I asked her how Sweaty Keith was. "Is he still sweating?"

"Don't be mean, Maisy!" she snapped, before she bowed her head and admitted that he still tended to perspire quite a bit. "You know he has funny glands."

"He's not the only one. Dave's anal glands are dripping all over the carpet."

"What? Your Dad's fag man?"

"No! Our dog."

"Oh, of course. That flea ridden pest."

Mum doesn't like my dog. She has a Pom dog called Saffy - that is, a high class pooch and not in the same league as our mongrel. Apparently, Sweaty Keith was out walking him while we were having our meal. Quite a thought in itself, as Sweaty Keith is six foot tall and six foot wide and the dog is a fuzzy white fur ball on legs (complete with pink bow).

As we left, Mum squeezed a twenty into my hand.

"But don't give it to the Leech," she hissed.

She also made me promise that I would attend Sweaty Keith's 50th birthday, which she was trying to arrange. A party contained in their pokey one-bedroom flat! The thought makes me cringe. Poor Keith's glands will be under even more pressure.

I'm worried they might blow…

*Comments*

**JesseBelle:** Aw, I do love your Mum. She's a nutter like mine x

**MaisyM:** Difference is, your Mum stuck around

**JesseBelle:** True. But then again she wasn't married to your Dad ;0)

Good luck with the recruitment agency tomorrow, text me and let me know how you get on x

**Friday 29th July 2011**

**Recruit4You (or as I like to call them…. Screw You)**

Ollie is already really starting to do my head in. He is still sat on the sofa opposite Dad, and hasn't bothered to do anything! Oh, I tell a lie – he has had a bath and changed out of his suit and into a pair of jeans and T-shirt. And I might have actually seen him wash a mug yesterday – but apart from that…

He did buy Dad a present (it's only a few days late I suppose) – a bottle of wine. Dad doesn't do wine. He sniffed it suspiciously and then stuffed it in the back of the cupboard. Dad thinks wine is for 'posh people.'

He looked at me with scorn when I was leaving to go to the recruitment agency.

"Have fun," Ollie cackled. "I wonder what fantastic temping jobs they will find you? Hardly a boom time! You'd be lucky to find a job cleaning bogs."

"And what exactly are you doing today?" I said.

"I'm going to the Pride later with Dad." He had the cheek to answer.

"It'll be nice having you with me, son," Dad added. "Stops me having to talk to all those other drunken weirdos."

"I thought you were meant to be starting your new project? We need money if you're to stay here," I told him.

Ollie smiled again. "And I will. I'm waiting for that ex of mine to bring my stuff down, as she's kindly said she would. I can't do much without my laptop, now, can I?"

I said no more, I wasn't volunteering my computer for his use. I'd never get it back.

Instead I did a very childish, and quite a girly thing. I slammed the door as I left. I'm sure I heard him sniggering behind me as I did it.

*God I hate him.*

By the time I was stood outside the bright pink building that is Recruit4You, I could feel a small amount of bile rising in my throat. I'm sure that is not the normal reaction. I usually feel that way when I eat pickled onions. I hate recruitment agencies; they look so scary and unapproachable and, let's face it, they don't look like the sort of place that would welcome an unemployed teenager with a handful of GCSE's.

Judy, my fairly fat and frumpy contact at the job centre, had stuffed their card into my hand after weeks of failing to find me work. It seems that lack of experience ruled me out of half of her jobs and having an ounce of ambition ruled me out of the others.

"I could get you some work in the CD factory," she whispered. "But I know its office work you want really."

I think she felt sorry for me. The last lot that they packed off to the CD factory could barely string a sentence together. One of them used to be in my Humanities class at school, before he dropped out. He used to spend the entire lesson drawing giant boobs on the wall (complete with strangely stretched out nipples). I don't really fancy being stuck on a minibus with him again.

But the truth is I may have to take any job offered soon. We have bills piling up around our eyes and barely enough food in the fridge to feed a gnat.

My pathetic one-page CV was clutched in my sweaty hand as I pushed open the frosted glass door and strode into a very small reception area. A tiny, blonde haired girl with piercing green eyes sat at an even tinier desk, typing furiously.

"I've come to register," my voice came out almost like a squeak.

She looked at me, a perfectly plucked eyebrow slightly raised. She seemed bored.

"Temp or perm?"

"Both"

She nodded as if she knew that would be the answer and carefully selected a form from the pile in front of her.

"Fill this in and I'll see what I can do."

She flapped her hand to indicate the chairs in front of her and then looked away to restart her typing. Her time with me was done. I glanced behind her and could see a few people sitting at desks – most were on the phone. One guy looked completely lost under a mound of paperwork.

I felt like I didn't belong here. There was an air of snobbery about the place that I didn't like. I wished that I had worn my one decent suit instead of my tatty jeans and skimpy pink top.

The form itself didn't take long – standard personal details, qualifications. I noted my GCSE's, six in total which I scraped through. I hated school and couldn't wait to leave. I'd once dreamed about going to College and studying further, but never mind. When you got a life like mine, you get used to things not going right.

Ollie is the successful one in our family. He was the one who got away and was making a fortune playing with pretend money. We never normally talk about Ollie's success though. It's almost like we're a little ashamed of *him*.

In the section that asked 'what type of role are you looking for' I scrawled 'anything,' because I am. I can't carry on cooking meals made from beans and super-noodles.

I wrote that I was a 'hardworking, dedicated girl with the ability to turn my hand to anything' and named my Saturday Job Manager and Stella Bridges (Jess's Mum) as my references.

I gave my form back to the snotty girl on reception, fairly pleased I had been so quick. She took the form carefully from my hand, as if it was contaminated. As she was checking both sides, her lips turned into a snarl.

"Hmmm....not got much experience then...," she said, not looking at me.

"A Saturday Job at a shoe shop, and I've helped out at a hair salon, washing hair and stuff." I could hear the desperation in my voice, "I *will* do anything."

"Well. My consultants are still busy at the moment."

Looking behind her shoulder, one woman was on the phone, another was re-applying her lipstick and the guy was clutching several handfuls of paper and looking utterly confused.

"I'll make you an appointment to see Dan," she sighed. "I'm sure he can help you."

Her tone had seemed sarcastic. Something told me she didn't like Dan almost as much as she didn't like me.

"Can't I see him now?" I asked, eager to get it over and done with

"That's not how it's done," she hissed back.

I left with a small pink card and an allotted time to see Dan next Monday at 10am.

As I left, I cast the man in question another glance. He'd thrown all of his paperwork on the floor and was resting his head on the desk.

I don't hold out much hope...

When I got home there was a pile of bin bags outside the house, with a great big sheet of a paper stuck on the top of it. Scrawled on the sheet, in black marker pen, it said:

**FOR THE CRAPHEAD!!! I HOPE YOU ROT IN HELL!!!**

It looks like Ollie has got his stuff back then.

# Comments

**Lucy Locket:** Hi – I found you on Twitter. Love your Blog. Good luck with the job search. I'm looking too

**MaisyM:** Thanks for commenting. Hopefully I will find something soon. How about you?

**Lucy Locket:** Just finished Uni. Not much around at mo. Will probably do some waitressing work to tide me over tho.

Good luck!

**MaisyM:** Thanks. You too.

**JesseBelle:** Ha Ha!! Poor Ollie – He's really messed up

Hope she ain't cut his stuff up?

**MaisyM:** I didn't dare look. Just left it outside his room. He's been out all day – Again!

God only knows where he goes x


## Saturday 30ᵗʰ July 2011

### Pride of Place

Tonight was a night down the Pride, with Jess and Poppy. My best mates. My pair of nutters.

It took me ages to get ready to come out tonight as I'm running out of stuff to wear. I had my entire wardrobe tipped out on the bed next to me and nothing looked right. I have the joys of inheriting my Dad's lanky body, all arms and legs. Clothes just hang off of me, looking shapeless and baggy. I'd kill for Mum's boobs (well, the ones she had in her twenties, the ones she has now aren't so pert and look more like deflated balloons…)

I stood for ages earlier, staring in the mirror. Looking critically at my face, like a jigsaw puzzle of my parent's bits and pieces. My Dad's greenish eyes, his long nose and my Mum's wide mouth and mousey hair. My hair wouldn't be so bad if I could afford to have highlights; it's so frizzy I have to wear it tied back all the time.

I know I'm not pretty. I'm what you would call well and truly average. A bit of make-up helps. But only a bit.

I finally settled on a red top and a pair of skinny jeans and left the house feeling fairly confident

Jess and Poppy were waiting for me outside the pub, moaning that I was late (I wasn't!)

It's rare that Poppy comes out these days so it's good to see her. I can write honestly about Poppy because

    a)   She can take it, and:
    b)   I wouldn't say anything about Poppy that she wouldn't say herself.

All Poppy wants in life is a good square meal (or five) and anything that relates to vampires or the un-dead. If she's not reading about them, she's watching a film about them. She would bloody sleep with one if she could. Honestly!

I love Poppy to bits and she is (as my Dad would say) a "lady of the larger nature" but she really doesn't mind being fat – she says it "adds to her character". The truth is she is absolutely gorgeous. She has the clearest skin I have ever seen and the most beautiful, long, red curly hair. She's like a goddess from the old days.

As for Jess, she is not so much pretty as striking. She has one of those large frames that could be seen as slightly overweight, but somehow she always manages to maximise her assets – skimming in her waist and thrusting out her rather large breasts. She also has a similar hair colour to me, but unlike me she has a mother who will happily bleach to it when required, so her long blonde hair is quite eye catching.

I'm not worried about Jess reading this as I know she would agree with all of the above, except she would moan about her piggy eyes and big nose (which is bloody nonsense if you ask me!)

It just goes to show we are never happy with our looks.

We sat ourselves in the corner of the pub. That's where Jimmy Brent (the landlord) lets us sit. He knows we are underage, but he's known Dad for years, so he turns a blind eye to us being there. Just as long as we stick to soft drinks.

"I could do with a shot of vodka in mine," Jess was moaning.

"Don't be daft, you know he'll notice," I hissed back.

"Yeah, yeah…I know. I was just saying."

I was immediately distracted because I saw Ollie was there. Not sitting with us, but propped up at the bar with one of his old school friends, Richard. I remembered that he used to come to our house and smoke in the bedroom. He still has a really spotty chin.

Ollie still looked pretty rough, but I don't suppose he cared about his bruises. Nobody would take any notice of them in here anyway. Every second bloke in this pub has been in one fight or another.

My heart dropped even further when I saw Dad was there too, at the corner of the bar. I really thought he had gone to Norm's tonight. I just hoped the girls wouldn't notice him.

Jess was in a foul mood because her boss had caught her smoking in the stockroom. She has been given a final warning. Apparently she came close to singeing a box of knickers. Jess had also noticed Ollie walk in and pissed me off a bit by telling me he was "well fit."

"I want to leave my job anyway," Jess was saying, sipping her drink. "I hate retail, it's so....so well, nothing. I want something more."

"I'd have anything," I replied.

"I know what I want." Poppy said, a small smile forming on her soft face. "I want my book to be the next bestseller. And then I would be world famous and Stu Maguire would fall helplessly in love with me."

Honestly, all Poppy goes on about is that soppy actor from 'Vampire High.' She's convinced he's the man of her dreams. She's either gassing on about him, or that book she's been writing for the last two years.

Poppy has no worries though; she is still at school coasting through her A Levels and her Dad is loaded (something in Property) so it's likely that she would never really have to work if she didn't want to. She could probably work on "her book" all her life if she wanted.

Poppy's Dad is one of those men that drives fast cars, wears beautiful designer suits and seems to have a certain charm oozing out him even though he is bald and has a bulging pot belly. Her Mum tends to hang on his every word like a hypnotised limpet. She is a strange mouse of a woman – and, like Poppy, lives her life through movies and romantic novels. Most of the time you could forget she was there, she is that quiet and unassuming.

I would love to have a Dad like Poppy's though. When he walks into the room, everyone takes notice. The same thing happens to me with my Dad these days, but for all the wrong reasons.

Unfortunately, tonight was another one of those nights when my Dad would be the one grabbing the attention. I had become more aware of my Dad as the evening progressed. He was sitting on his stool – well, kind of sitting. One buttock was on the seat and the other was hanging off. He was scratching the hanging buttock quite violently with his right hand. He looked just like a flea-ridden dog. A drunk, flea-ridden dog.

Dad was looking more and more wobbly on his bar stool and was pointing wildly at some bloke standing beside him (at least he had stopped scratching). This fella was not a regular; he was wearing a naff woolly jumper and badly fitting jeans.

Forgetting the girls' conversation for a moment, I wandered over to hear what was going on.

"You......you lot make me sick with your shooting!" My Dad slurred loudly.

The guy in question, who was obviously trying to order a drink, turned to my Dad and looked a bit confused.

"I don't know what you mean," he said, quite politely.

I walked over and squeezed myself between the pair. The man had a rosy, red face (a bit like my Dad's but for an altogether different reason) and his lips were wide and wet.

"What's going on?" I asked.

"Well. I was chatting to this...." The flabby lipped guy waved his hand at my father, barely able to give him a name. "And I happened to tell him that I had been shooting today."

"Oh!"

"Shooting poor defenceless birds!" My Dad interrupted. "Never did no harm to anyone, flapping harmlessly in the sky and this flashy-arse so-and-so comes along and shoots them out of the clouds!"

"No - You don't understand -" The man seemed quite pleased with himself now. "I don't shoot birds, I shoot at paper targets."

"Paper targets?" My dad now screamed, spittle flying freely. "That's even bloody worse! What a waste of time shooting pieces of paper when you could be shooting a useless bird or something!"

This was the moment when Ollie appeared from behind me and took the startled man's arm gently in his hand.

"Take no notice of him, no one does; he is quite mad," he said gently, flashing my Dad an apologetic smile. "Let me buy you another drink and take you away from his ranting."

And with such ease, he guided the bewildered man away, to the far side of the pub and into the safe hands of Jimmy Brent's wife, Alice.

"Your brother has charm, you know," my dad slurred, before resting his head on the bar.

I'd barely turned my back on him and there was an almighty crash. I turned to find my Dad in a heap on the floor, all arms and legs.

"I'm alright, I'm alright..." he slurred, pushing away imaginary helpers. Everyone was ignoring him, obviously too used to his antics. I watched as he slowly pulled himself up against the bar again, his skinny frame resting against the wood. He looked so old. So pathetic.

I left the pub soon after, unable to watch my dad's steady decline. I persuaded the girls to watch a DVD with me at Poppy's house, unable to face an evening at mine.

I came home at two a.m. to find Dad unconscious on the kitchen floor, his head resting in the fridge and his right foot resting in the dog bowl.

I did check his pulse, just to make sure he was still alive, and then I left him in that rather uncompromising position. It just wasn't worth the risk of the bruises and the verbal abuse that I would undoubtedly receive if I attempted to shift him.

At first I thought that Ollie was out or in bed, but as I turned to go upstairs, I suddenly realised that he was sitting, quite still, in the living room. In pitch darkness.

"Ollie, are you okay?" I asked

But he didn't answer, didn't even move. That's just bloody typical. I bet he was drunk as well. I decided to leave him to it.

Honestly, something has to get me out of this house before I go nuts.


## Comments

**JesseBelle:** It was fun tonight, gr8 to c u girls again. Pops is so funny.

Don't worry about your Dad or Ollie, families are hard work (I should know) p.s when you left Pops joined a Stu Maguire fansite – sad !!! bless her ;o)

**MaisyM:** Thanks. I'll try not to worry

**JesseBelle:** ...And Ollie is fit. Where have you been hiding him?

**MaisyM:** OY! He's too old for you! And he's an arsehole! And you love Steve.

**JesseBelle:** Yeah, yeah..lol xx


## Sunday 31st July 2011

### Ollie and Mum

Mum called this morning to check that I was still OK to come for Sunday dinner. I was really hoping that this would be a chance for me to escape and be with people that *weren't* my Dad and my brother. But, of course, Ollie appeared from nowhere and snatched the phone off me.

"Mum!" He yelled in fake joy. "It's been so long. Guess who's come home!"

"Ollie!" I heard her screech from where I was standing. It could've easily shattered an eardrum.

"So where is Maz going?" he asked. Secretly, I was praying that Mum would suddenly forget that she had wanted Ollie to come for dinner too. I was praying that she might suffer some form of early dementia and maybe even forget who Ollie was.

I watched as Ollie turned to face me, a small smile creeping over his face.

"Really? No...No, Maz never told me. Maybe she forgot?" He looked at me and winked; he knew. He knew I didn't want him there. "Dinner sounds lovely. I'd love to come as well!"

Aaaarghhh!!!

Walking to Mums with Ollie was painful. It's not a long journey by any means, but when you are walking alongside someone you actually despise each step is an agonising and torturous one.

Ollie is just over five years older than me. Mum and Dad had him when they were first married, in their early flushes of love. And he was a beautiful-looking boy – I've seen the pictures. Mum always goes on about how much of an angel he was, how sweet and tender he was – such a mummy's boy.

26

It took them ages to have me, by which time they had given up. Mum thought I was a stomach bug, because she was having loads of cramp-like pains. Instead it turned out it was the implantation of little, old me disturbing her womb lining (what a lovely thought). Apparently, Dad went on a three day bender with his mate Norm to celebrate.

Trouble is, a five-and-a-half year old boy who has been the centre of attention for so long, doesn't like it much when a new baby comes along.

One of my earliest memories is of Ollie shutting me in the wardrobe and telling me to stay there or the goblins would come and bite off my nose. I was only about two. I still remember crouching in the dark and the smell of old clothes hanging against my face as I sat there shaking, not even sure what a bloody goblin was!

Ollie hated me. He would steal my toys, pinch my chubby arms, break my dolls and flush their heads down the toilet. And if I went crying to Mum, he'd be even worse the next day. I soon learnt it was best to keep my mouth closed and put up with it.

Things were a bit better when he hit thirteen. I became less interesting and he just ignored me. I just became a slight irritation, like a buzzing bluebottle in the room that every so often would be slapped away.

Luckily for me though, he was already charming the girls with his dazzling good looks and was rarely home. He left for good after his A Levels, moving up to London to kip on some mate's floor, blagging job after job, slowly climbing his way up the career ladder. He is smart and very quick. He's also ruthless and doesn't care whose toes he steps on along the way,

We last saw him three years ago when he made a fleeting visit, after he heard Mum had left. He stayed for a few hours, took Dad out for a few drinks and was gone again. If you blinked you would have missed him.

Family is only of interest to Ollie when he needs something.

Walking beside me now, Ollie was rummaging in his jacket, obviously looking for a cigarette. He still looked pretty rough. He needed a shave and I noticed that his hair was getting very long at the back.

"So, why do you think you won't go back to Lottie?" I asked, trying to make conversation.

"Lottie is a handful."

He stopped walking and bent down to light his fag. The wind was whipping at his hair – making him look quite wild and jaded.

"The fact is she wouldn't take me back," he said quite softly.

"What did you do?"

Ollie turned to face me, his eyes glinting. "Why the hell would I tell you, Maz? You couldn't even begin to understand."

We carried on in silence for the rest of the five-minute journey. I was so relieved to reach the battered All-Day Café and scamper up the stairs that ran alongside it.

"What a hell hole," Ollie muttered behind me. "Dad said she's with a right fat twat now – is that true?"

"Not sure 'fat' is the right word," I replied. "But he is quite big boned."

Banging at the door, I could hear Saffy yapping and jumping up against the frame. She hates visitors. Within seconds Mum was there, all hair and arms (quite literally, she has a new spiky hair-do – I'm not sure it suits her thin face to be honest, she looks a bit like a broom head now).

"Ollie," she yelled, totally ignoring me. I slipped in quietly, stroked the nutty dog and went to find Sweaty Keith, sitting in his usual place on the sofa.

Saffy, however, obviously didn't like the smell of arseholes either. I heard the scream and the sound of growls (strangely from both Ollie and the dog) and walked back in the hall to find the fluffy fur ball attached firmly to Ollie's left ankle.

"Get this vicious ball of fluff off my leg," he was screaming, jerking it back and forth. Saffy was hanging on like a limpet, her beady eyes gleaming with determination.

Suddenly, with one forceful jerk, he managed to flip Saffy off and up into the air like a giant snowball.

I stood there watching her, hurtling in slow motion, until she was smartly caught at the other end of the hall by a calm but disgruntled Sweaty Keith.

"Nobody kicks my dog!" he muttered, before taking his pampered pooch back into the living room.

"Never mind, dear!" Mum was telling Ollie, who was busy rubbing his sore leg. "I'm sure she'll come to love you eventually."

"Bloody lethal weapon that thing is!" he moaned back.

Back in the living room, Sweaty Keith was soothing his pooch by tenderly singing "How much is that Doggy in Window". Saffy, to be honest, was not looking impressed.

"That bloody brother of yours. Who does he think he is, kicking a poor defenceless little dog?" Sweaty Keith complained to me. "Not the best first impression to make, is it?"

Ollie glared at him as he walked into the room and said nothing. I noticed that he continued to rub his leg.

It's hardly surprising that particular dinner was a muted affair. Mum was obviously delighted to have her darling son home again. Unsurprisingly, Sweaty Keith took objection to Ollie, especially as Mum gave him the extra Yorkshire pudding. I could see the look of hatred forming in the big man's eyes.

Suddenly I'm beginning to like Sweaty Keith a little bit more.

## Comments

**JesseBelle:** Ha ha – that made me pee my knickers a bit. I can't believe that fur-ball attacked him!

**Lucy Locket:** This was very funny, I don't know if I feel more sorry for the dog or your brother.

**MaisyM:** The dog, trust me, the dog!

## Monday 1st August

## Dan, Dan, Recruitment Man

Today was appointment day with the shaggy-haired chap at Recruit4You. Considering I had only eaten a packet of Wotsits for breakfast, I was hoping that this man would help me find a job sooner rather than later.

Dad was no longer in the kitchen when I left the house; he was now back in his armchair, resting his legs on a sorrowful-looking Dave and moaning about his sore back.

"I could be dying," he was groaning to me, or Dave. I think the dog was more concerned.

"Possibly," I replied, pulling my coat out from under his bum. "But knowing my luck, probably not."

"You're a heartless cow. You don't know what it's like to suffer!"

"You've got a hangover, Dad. That's not suffering, it's punishment."

As a contrast, my evening had consisted of two Cokes, a kebab and a late night film with Poppy (soppy and mind-numbing). What an exciting life! I thought teenagers were meant to be the delinquent ones?

"If Dave's bum starts to dribble again, there's some Dettol under the sink!"

My Dad's legs shot off the dogs back as if he was diseased. "You can piss off!" he sneered at Dave (who was now looking rather confused.) "Bloody thing needs a cork up his rectum!"

"He needs a vet, and that's why I'm trying to get some cash together!"

I stormed out of the house, leaving him ranting about 'crappy animals' and 'smelly arses.' I suppose it takes one to know one.

I rushed to my appointment, desperately picking Dave's hairs from my jacket and worrying that I smelt like dog. I didn't have the money for the bus, so I looked up at the looming grey clouds, prayed hard for the sun to make an appearance and power-walked into town. When I walk fast, I always look like someone whose knickers are wedged up their bum. It's not a very cool look.

Snotty Sue was still on the desk when I arrived at the agency, so unfortunately my silent curse to have her fall under a runaway bus didn't work then…What a shame…

"*Miss* Malone?" she said, but there was no inflection in her question. She knew who I was. Her eyes darted over my jacket (which I admit had seen better days) and she smirked. "Dan will be with you shortly."

She flapped her hand once again at the seating area. I sat myself down next to a tall, blonde woman, who was wearing bright red shoes. She was in a suit and clutching a portfolio on her lap. I had never felt so young and inadequate. This woman smelt of flowers and expense. She did not smell of dog.

The Consultants looked as though they were in the same position as last week; one was still on the phone, another was typing, whilst slowly leafing through some paperwork and the guy, Dan, was texting. I wondered if they had actually been to bed at all that night. Maybe their whole lives existed within the portals of their desks. Certainly the elfin-faced one with the sulky mouth seemed permanently attached to her stupid phone.

Beside me were some business magazines. Not knowing what else to do, I picked one up. The front cover showed a woman running on a beach clutching a briefcase, long red hair streaming behind her, her crisp shirt and suit not dissimilar to the woman beside me. The tagline read, "how to have it all."

I flipped to the relevant page and scanned the bullet points suggesting how you could achieve this:-

*'Utilise the support, skills and resources that those close to you, such as your family, can provide.'*

I closed the magazine again.

"Hello,"

I looked up and saw Dan the Consultant standing up behind his desk. He beckoned to me to come over. His mop of dark hair looked like it needed a brush, and he had day-old stubble, but his eyes were blue and sparkling. He didn't look that old though, younger than Ollie if I had to guess.

I walked over to his desk. It was still piled high with CVs, application forms and random sheets of paper. Dan grabbed the top form, which I presumed was mine, and gestured for me to sit down on the chair opposite.

Dan was looking at my form like my Maths teacher used to look at my homework; there was a degree of sympathy in his expression. Almost a 'you poor thing, is this all you have to show me' look.

"OK. I know its rubbish," I blurted. "But I really will do anything. The Job Centre is next to useless; I have to wait for benefits and all the while I have responsibilities."

"Children?" Dan asked, looking surprised.

"Oh...no, not that!" God what a thought, although Sharon Henderson is my age and she has two under five now..... "No – I have a lazy parent and a stinky dog"

Dan nodded. "I understand. I have similar problems..." He smiled at me and I noticed the slight gap between his front teeth; they were slightly crooked too in a cute sort of way.

"Do you have any other skills or interests?"

"Er, well, I like writing. I'm even keeping a blog at the moment."

"Really?" He raised an eyebrow.

"Yeah, I mean it's nothing exciting, just about my life and stuff. Probably only my best mate reads it. But I use a fake name, Maisy Malone, just in case I upset anyone."

He laughed. "It sounds interesting."

I sat back while he tapped hopefully at his computer looking for something for me. I noticed a photo frame on his desk, a picture of him and a pretty girl clinking glasses. The girl looked familiar. Dan saw me looking.

"Aw - that's me and Sadie on our holiday in Crete. Sadie works here too, look!"

Of course, when he pointed her out I recognised Sadie as one of the other consultants, the one always on the phone. This time she was looking right at me, her elfin cropped hair and small green eyes were staring hard at us, making her appear quite evil.

"Ah-ha!" Dan declared pointing at the screen. "I think I've found something. Now really this should be for someone more experienced, but sod it, I like you. And how experienced do you have to be to do a bit of filing and make some coffee?"

"I make the best coffee!" I told him enthusiastically.

"Well. I'm afraid it doesn't start for a week or so. Their current person is working their notice and they need someone to help out until the permanent replacement starts. But it should be for a few weeks." Dan shuffled through his paperwork. "I'm afraid I haven't got anything else until then."

"That's ok, I'll be glad of anything at the moment to be honest. The news is full of youth unemployment. My Dad says it's worse than the eighties."

Dan laughed. "I wouldn't know. But it is pretty hard going at the moment. Hopefully things will pick up soon."

So, I left his office with my first assignment lined up as an office junior for this small graphic design company across town – MJ Design. I haven't heard of them before but I imagine that they would be highly professional and have nice, swanky offices.

I could've hugged Dan afterwards, but I think Scary Sadie may have killed me.

Just wait until I tell old smug-face Ollie. Cleaning bogs. Yeah right. This is the start of great things, I just know it.


## Comments

**JesseBelle:** YEAAAAAAAAA!!!!! Well done babes. I so chuffed for you.

**Lucy Locket:** Well done, that's fab news.

That Dan is a diamond. You should celebrate

**MaisyM:** No funds to celebrate ;o(

**Popsicle:** It's great news babe. You will be an office girl now

**007:** New follower! Just wanted to say hi and congratulations. Sounds like you deserve it.

**MaisyM:** Thank you


## Tuesday 2nd August 2011

### Teddy Bear

I've been beaming all day today, I just can't help myself. Little old me has got a job, a proper job.

Even Dad was pleased. He actually made me a cup of tea! I can't remember the last time he did that. I think it might have been when Granddad died.

Ollie has been in his room for most of the day. I saw him briefly at breakfast, while I was buttering my toast. I told him my news and he just grunted into his cornflakes.

"Aren't you pleased for me?" I asked

He wouldn't even look at me, he just kept stabbing at his soggy cereal.

"It's a temp job, Maz," he muttered. "What's the fuss? There are far more important things to get stressed about."

I stood there with the butter knife in my hand, seriously wondering if it would fit up his right nostril.

Why is he so horrible?

He sloped off back to his room minutes later, leaving me his bowl to clean up. I was so angry I followed him, intending to have a go at him for being so lazy.

But when I got to his room and peered around the door, I saw that he was bent over something. Peering closer I could see it was that pink teddy bear that I found in his room the other day.

But what made it worse was that he was crying. Crying over a stupid bear.

I crept away quickly, feeling really uncomfortable.

I swear he's not right in the head

## Comments

**Lucy Locket:** Aw bless him. He must be really cut up about that girl. Poor thing

**MaisyM:** Hmm Maybe

**JesseBelle:** Either that – or he has done something really bad!!

**007:** You are too hard on him, give him a bit of space. Sounds like he's hurting. And people that have been hurt always strike out.

**MaisyM:** Wise words – thank you

**007:** No problem. Look beyond the stuff that annoys you. He is your brother after all.

**MaisyM:** Okay Mr Advice Man – I will

**007:** Not an 'Advice Man' – just a man. We're not all bad ;o)


## Thursday 4th August

### A Present For the Sweaty One

Mum had phoned to remind me about Sweaty Keith's party on Saturday.

"You must come. It's his 50th! He's so excited, bless him. And make sure you buy him something nice."

Now this last request posed a problem because:

a) I have no money
b) I really can't think of anything nice I want to buy him.

I mean, what do you buy for a man who is sweaty, hairy and only talks about music (nothing post 1985), motorbikes and fish.

I debated buying him another book on fish, but as he is a self-confessed expert (and quite honesty a bore) on all things aquatic – I know that this would no doubt be sold at their next car boot sale.

I can't afford anything motorbike-related. It's not like you can buy something small and cheap to go with a bike, like a fancy air freshener or a nodding dog. Everything is either big or leathery.

And as for music - I'm not making that mistake again. I bought him the best of Duran Duran last year and he actually (although quite nicely) told me it was the crappiest thing anyone had every given him. Mum later told me that the lead singer, Simon Le Bon, once stood on his toe outside a club in Soho and he never even apologised. Sweaty Keith said, "He had the air of a man who spent too long smelling the scent of his own backside." But of course that's just his opinion, I'm sure he's a really nice person really…

The Duran Duran CD is now being used as a coaster by their bed, so I guess it has a use (of sorts). Poor Simon Le Bon now has a nasty ring of tea on his forehead; it looks a bit like a stained halo. It's a shame really as I think he looks like quite a nice bloke, even though he has a dodgy haircut – he looks like he's been at it with my Nanna's hedge-trimmer.

I asked Ollie if he wanted to 'come in with me' on the present, but he just laughed.

"I barely know the guy," he shrugged. "I'll just bring some cans to the party."

"Oh, so you are coming then?"

"Of course I am. I wouldn't miss it for the world."

I'm surprised actually. Ollie has never been known to attend family gatherings. I think he's trying to keep on Mum's good side, but I'm not sure why. I'm sure he's up to something.

Anyway, I knew I had to buy Sweaty Keith something, so (mainly because I couldn't be bothered to go any further) I ended up in Hussain's Corner Shop, buying his Special Promotion Linx-like box-set. It looked a bit knocked about if I'm honest, like a mouse might have chewed one of the corners of the packaging, but the fragrance was "essence of man" and if anyone needs to have a new essence it's Sweaty Keith.

I do wonder what "essence of man" would be. My experience of men admittedly is limited to my Dad (who smells stale, beery and sometimes a little like that strange blue cheese), Sweaty Keith (sweat, strangely enough), boys at school (who all stank of cheap aftershave and hormones) and Ollie.

Ollie always seems to smell lovely, but then Ollie will be six hours in the bathroom, spend thirty quid on face creams and even more on his hair.

My Dad calls him a 'poof,' but I think he's a bit scared of him. All I know is that he may smell nice, but he's still an arsehole.

I also managed to find Sweaty Keith a cheap card in Hussain's shop. It had a big fat 50 on it and a picture of a chubby guy trudging up a hill. The man on the card looked a bit like Sweaty Keith, except that he had a huge droopy moustache. The message inside read:

*"Enjoy the view while you can - it's all downhill from here....!"*

That should cheer him up nicely. If I brought my Mum a card like that, she would flee the house screaming and book herself into the first plastic surgery clinic she could find. Sweaty Keith won't react that badly, but he might pour himself another whiskey and start moaning about "the good old days."


## Comments

**JesseBelle:** We're coming btw, Pops text me earlier to say she would. There's no Vampire movie on that night obviously. Hope there will be some tasty men there!

**MaisyM:** Are you joking!! This is Sweaty's party – anyway what about Steve?

**JesseBelle:** What about him? He keeps following these random girls on Twitter – it's doing my head in.

**007:** What is essence of man then? I'm not sure I have an essence...

**MaisyM:** I can get you some too if you like! It's on offer at Hussains

**007:** I might hold you to that


## Saturday 6th August 2011

## Party Time

I have just come back from Sweaty Keith's party. Oh, what an event that was. On one side of the room were fifteen or so biker blokes squashed into the corner, munching mini sausages and an Indian platter selection that my mother had carefully laid out, complete with tiny sprigs of parsley.

Most of Sweaty Keith's mates look like they should be at a Status Quo concert (sadly I know of this band as my Nan, bless her, is a huge fan). If you haven't heard of them, Google it – and don't blame me for what you find ;o)

On the other side of the room was me, Jess (who agreed to come as a favour), my mum dressed in the tightest trousers I had ever seen and her friend Rene. Rene is mum's only friend; she is too high maintenance to have many people close to her. And Rene can't get too close to my Mum because her great big boobs get in the way. They look like something out of a magazine and are so high up they seem to push her all out of proportion.

"It's the best thing I ever did girls," she told us, whilst sucking on her mini kebab. "I feel lifted."

"So do your nipples," Jess shot back. "They must have a great view of the ceiling."

Jess was in another foul mood. Her boyfriend Steve has been spending a lot of time on his new phone, mainly on internet sites. Jess has noticed that he's been chatting to a lot of new followers, all of them female.

"He says it's to do with football and Crystal Palace," she said. "But how come he keeps giggling and hiding his phone from me? I doubt he's talking about the off-side rule."

I just shrugged. It's no secret that I think Steve is a bit of a knob. And a bloody thick one at that. I know Jess could do so much better.

"Maybe you should have a break from him?" Poppy suggested.

She had just wandered back from the buffet with a plate laden with greasy delights; it was actually buckling under the weight. She picked up a soggy nugget and waved it at me.

"I've been chatting to Ollie over there," she told me, pointing her nugget towards the man in question. I could see Ollie standing there, laughing with a man with an extraordinarily long, greasy ponytail. "He's so funny. He was telling me all sorts of stories."

"Really?" I sneered in his direction.

"Yes, really. He was telling about the time you used to eat the dog food, when you were little."

"How sweet of him..." I could feel myself getting more frustrated.

"Aw Maisy, leave him alone," Jess said, peering over at him. "He is so cute. How can something so fit be so bad?"

"You know nothing. Who are you to judge anyway? The girl that dates idiots?..."

"Yeah, well, I was only saying... anyway, your mum's got camel toe," Jess hissed back, obviously annoyed with me.

"Eh?"

I looked around and, to my horror, saw for myself that my mother's supposedly sexy trousers were now snaking up and creating a very definite and horrific crease between her legs.

I distracted myself by wandering over to the drinks table and pouring myself another fruit cocktail. One of Sweaty Keith's cling-ons was stood there. He was young, not much older than me and, unlike most of the others, he had short cropped hair.

Actually he was very good looking.

"I'm Keith's nephew, Adam," he said. "Do you remember?"

I tried to think back to the last family 'get-together' but nothing came to mind, so I shook my head uselessly.

"Your Dad tried to thump Keith and ended up falling head first into the bins?"

"Aw! Charlotte's Christening!"

Charlotte was another niece or cousin of Sweaty Keith's (he has a huge family) who had a christening about two years ago. It would have been fine if they hadn't chosen to have a few drinks afterwards, at the Pride....

I still didn't remember Adam though. I'm now thinking he must have been the sullen, spotty boy glued to his Mum's side the whole time. He's certainly changed!

Adam was okay actually, we chatted for a bit and although he bored me a bit when he talked about Star Wars, he seemed quite normal. I didn't stay with him for long as I could feel Poppy's evil eyes burn into me and realised that she was being chatted up by some fat, forty-something wearing a Spiderman T-shirt.

As I slipped back over to her, she hissed "cow," and then, "he was tasty" (Adam, not the man with the Spiderman T-shirt who was now trying to pick out lint from his belly button). So I think I was forgiven.

"Where's Jess?" I asked

Poppy pointed over to the other side of the room. There she was, chatting to Ollie, laughing in fact. One hand was resting on his arm. I recognised her body language, Jess was flirting.

"Oh no, not Ollie." I whispered. "He's too old. He's too horrible."

Poppy sniggered. "Jess doesn't think so."

It was never going to be a fantastic evening though, let's face it. The food was turning stale, the music was beyond crap (there is only so much eighties stuff that I can stand) and the flat itself was beginning to smell. It obviously wasn't designed to hold so many sweaty, male bodies. Even worse, my mother's trousers were creeping higher and higher...

All the time, Ollie and Jess were chatting in the corner. Standing very close.

Then at eleven, Sweaty Keith gave a loud cough which at first I thought was a belch. With the amount of barjis he had consumed this wouldn't have surprised me.

"Ladies and gents, can I have your attention please?" he said, all formal. He doesn't talk that much and it was unusual to hear him be so direct.

"I would like to thank you all for being here with me on my special day. And most of all I would like to thank my wife-to-be, Babs, for organising it all."

There was a pause: did we hear him right? Did he say wife-to-be? Suddenly the penny dropped and behind me Mum screamed and dropped her glass.

Sweaty Keith grinned and slowly went down on one knee. I realised that in his hand was a ring. It looked like one of the ones you win at the slot machines at Brighton.

"Aw Keith....you are so ROMANTIC!" She screamed – and then she literally leapt on him, legs either side of his rather large body. It was a miracle that he remained upright.

We all heard the rip. It was a painfully loud and quite comical sound. I almost couldn't bring myself to look, but I did.

All that evening I was worried about a crease between her legs - and now for the whole room to see, was her white, wobbly bottom.

I can't get the image of that out of my head even now. And my biggest worry is: will mine end up looking that fleshy and dimpled?

And my other biggest worry is... is my best mate getting too close to my brother? I ended up leaving before them. I don't even want to know what happened

## Comments

**Popsicle:** Stop worrying hun. At least you have a wedding to look forward to

And the man in the Spiderman T-shirt wasn't that bad, he was just a bit strange...bless him

**JesseBelle:** Yes stop worrying!!!!! We're just mates. He's a really nice guy.

I like him, get over it!

**MaisyM:** He's not as nice as you think he is

**JesseBelle:** He's not as bad as you think he is. Give him a chance

**Lucy Locket:** Don't fall out over a boy – not worth it!

Congratulations for your Mum btw – poor her, showing her bum!

**007:** Yeah, we're not worth falling out over. We smell (apparently ;o)

Sounded like a great party. I want to meet your Mum and the man in the Spiderman T-shirt

**MaisyM:** Ha ha, whoever you are – you are very strange for wanting that!

**007:** Not strange. Just interesting.


## Sunday 7th August

### Nanna

Today I decided to go and visit my Nanna. I've not seen her for a while and if I'm honest, I've missed her.

Nanna lives a bus ride away in a big old house that is crumbling around her. She refuses to move as she claims that this would be admitting defeat. She also says, weirdly, that "Johnny" (Gramps) is still with her. I'm not sure why this is a good thing – all Gramps used to do was nag at her when he was alive and she used to call him "the moaning old bastard" behind his back. It's funny how these things get glossed over when someone dies.

But now, Nanna is obsessed with Spiritualism and mediums. She watches Colin Fry and Sally Morgan on catch-up TV all day long and goes to physic "circles" most weeks. I don't think she's much good at it herself (she can barely hear the living) but she likes to have a go. Dad says it's because she is closer to death, she wants to make some friends "up there."

"It's the only friends she'll ever have – batty old bint!" he shouted at me last time I went to see her. "At least they don't have to put up with her fishy breath! She killed poor Johnny with the stench of kippers!"

Dad and Nanna don't get along. She never approved of the "lanky traffic warden" that my mum brought home one day and rightly predicted that a "surly little pratt like that would never keep my Mum happy…" Dad objects to her opinionated views and her liking for cooking fish (he does have a point about the kippers, they do whiff a bit).

Nanna still wasn't impressed when Mum ran off with the Man with the Long Nose and then Sweaty Keith. I think she hoped her daughter would be the strong, independent type, not someone who goes from man to man like a dose of flu.

The only thing my Dad and Nanna agree on is politics. They both hate the Tories and always spout on about that Thatcher woman, even though she died like ten years ago. Oh no, she didn't die, did she? That was the Queen Mother! I just know that they are both posh with funny hair.

When I arrived today, Nanna was standing proudly in her kitchen looking smug, so I knew she had been up to something. She's only 5ft1, but she always holds herself really tall and she piles her grey hair on her head in a heap to add height. A lot of people (including Mum) are quite scared of her.

I noticed that there was a great big sign behind her, lying sliced in two on the kitchen floor. It was one of those 'Vote Conservative' signs; it certainly didn't belong in this house.

"Oh Nanna – what have you done?" I asked straight away.

"Stupid knob head next door erected it next to my garden gate," she replied stoutly. "So I took my hedge-trimmer to it."

"But Nanna – that's criminal damage!"

"It's criminal damage what those idiots have done to this country! It's criminal damage to my eyes to have to look at that monstrosity every time I water my geranium," she spat back, giving the sign a quick kick, as if it was a naughty dog.

She was clearly on a rant. Her eyes were starting to do the mad bulging thing that always scared me a bit as kid. I used to worry that one might actually pop out, like those joke ones you get on plastic glasses.

I quickly made her cup of tea to calm her down, and led her into the living room, while she muttered about the unmentionable damage she would like to inflict on David Cameron.

Her attention was soon diverted in the living room when I noticed a leaflet on her coffee table; she had obviously left it out for me to see. She pushed it towards me, in case her intentions had not been clear enough – I couldn't help but look at her wrinkly old hands. I'm sure they are getting more aged every time I see them, and why do they keep getting those weird liver spot things? Dad is starting to get them too. They freak me out. It looks as if the skin is slowly rotting from inside, like a bruised apple.

I cast my eyes down at the creased leaflet. It was bright yellow and had a photo of a man with dodgy, long, permed hair. His arms were raised, as if he was praising the Lord or shouting abuse at him like Dad does. The words below said:

## KEV KIRBY – MEDIUM TO THE DEAD

## HE WILL AMAZE. HE WILL UNITE.

"Medium to the dead? What other types of medium are there, Nanna?" I asked (although thinking about it, getting someone to communicate with Dad would be pretty amazing).

She didn't answer, her lips were tightly pursed. I forgot that I wasn't allowed to criticise.

Kev Kirby (who sounded more like a dodgy singer my Mum would work with) was performing at the local Spiritualist Church next Saturday.

"You want me to go?" I asked softly.

She nodded. "Please Maisy. I'm hoping he might have a message for me."

I agreed on the condition that she would make me dinner that evening, and it wouldn't be kippers. I couldn't eat anything that smelt as if it had been dug out from the bin.

"I hear Ollie's home..." she muttered at me. "I don't suppose the smarmy so-and-so will bother to pay me a visit?"

"I'm not sure, Nanna, I don't see him much."

"Useless boy. He's probably forgotten I'm still alive. Your Mum thinks the sun shines out of his peachy bottom though."

I nodded. I think I'm more like my Nanna than anyone else in this stupid family.

The rest of the evening was spent smashing up Nanna's Tory sign into smaller bits and building a small bonfire in her back garden. She even threw one of Mum's old dolls on it, to act as a "guy".

"I'll pretend it's that cow, Maggie Thatcher," she hissed into the flames. "That woman killed this country's spirit with her greedy agenda and shiny black handbags"

We watched the bonfire for a bit, breathing in the smell of smoke.

"I feel so sorry for you," my Nanna said, suddenly. "What have you poor youngsters got? No jobs, no hope of your own house, benefits being scrapped, extortionate university fees, Tories back in power....If I was young I would be demonstrating on the streets."

"It's not so bad, Nanna," I replied meekly "I've got a temporary job now. Things are looking up."

"Temporary job? Well it's something I suppose. But how long will that last? And how many poor sods have nothing but benefits to look forward to?"

I left her house feeling pretty depressed. And, even worse, I couldn't afford a chocolate bar to cheer myself up.

Roll on start date.


## Comments

**Lucy Locket:** Your Nanna is dead right, she should be an MP.

**MaisyM:** Don't tell her that, you might encourage her!!

**BrendaWonderMum:** I am a medium and can I just say that we do an amazing job, contacting the dead and providing healing to many. Find out more on my website www.healinghandsandfeet.net

**MaisyM:** I'm sure you do an amazing job, but I don't want to be healed thank you

I will get my Dad to have a look at your site ;o)

**007:** You should get your Dad to go along to a reading, that'll be right up his street

I love the sound of your Nanna. Can I borrow her?

**MaisyM:** No!! She's all mine ;o)


**Monday August 8th 2011**

**Croydon's Burning….**

I was up in my room earlier this evening, typing on this stupid slow computer, when Jess sent me a message on Facebook:

*"Have you seen what's goin' on in town? Crazy riots, man."*

Flicking through the internet, the sites were full of it. People going crazy in the city, smashing windows, setting cars alight. Apparently it all kicked off because this guy got shot by police in Tottenham and a protest march that followed was boycotted by a group of rioters. This is the second night of rioting in London, but the first time it had crept outside to the suburbs.

Another message pinged up:

*"It's kicking off here. Fires everywhere…scary stuff."*

I went downstairs and found Dad comatose in his chair. The TV was on but it was an old repeat of Top Gear being replayed on one of the cable channels. I quickly switched it over to the news.

"Dad!" I kicked his shin. "Dad, look they're out on the streets again."

Dad woke up grumbling, dribble forming in the corner of his mouth. He looked like a demented gargoyle.

"What..? Eh…?" His eyes adjusted to the TV. "Jesus alive! Is that Croydon?"

We live in South Croydon in a three-bed terrace which really has seen better days. Living here has had its fair share of trouble, but nothing on this scale. We were suddenly aware of the sirens outside, the drone of the helicopters, only being slightly drowned out by the ridiculous volume my Dad has the TV. It's lucky the neighbours on one side are deaf and the other side aren't worth worrying about (that one is so shifty he would steal from his own mum).

"Some of them are just kids…" He shook his head sadly. "These are bad times."

Ollie came in the room, from his bedroom. His hair stuck up on end and huge bags sagged under his eyes. I swear he spends most of the day asleep.

"Have you heard...?" he stopped mid-sentence, his eyes falling on events being played out on the TV. "My God, it's worse than I thought. They really are wrecking the place!"

There was something so surreal about sitting there, with my Dad and Ollie, watching events that were unfolding outside our own front door.

Every so often Dad would comment or shake his head, or even worse recognise one of the looters (we felt sure we saw our mad neighbour running amok in a clothes shop) – but he was right, most of them were young. Many were my age.

I kept thinking about what Nanna had said to me. How she had said that 'youngsters had nothing' and how she wouldn't blame them for taking action. I'm not sure that putting a TV through the window of Curry's was Nanna's idea of 'taking action' though.

It felt weird that this was happening just outside the house, it was scary even. I was aware of how unsettled everything had suddenly become.

I wondered if I should be out there with them, screaming and smashing up shops. Angry because I couldn't afford university, angry because I couldn't get a job, angry because I had no hope of moving out of this poxy house. But I knew that I wouldn't. I knew that smashing things up wasn't going to make things any better.

And anyway, these people weren't angry.

"They're just knobs," my dad said, interrupting my thoughts.

And they were – he was dead right. I could tell my Dad was frustrated.

Before, when Mum was still home, Dad was a man of order – he believed in upholding the rule of law and took his job as a traffic warden extremely seriously. Some say too seriously.

Even so, I couldn't help but suppress a smile when we looked out of the window and saw a little, old lady running past our house clutching a handful of trainers. For one thing; who would have thought she would have been involved in looting and for another, why did she loot trainers? She was hardly Kelly Holmes.

"Do you need those to run from the grim reaper, do you?" my dad shouted out at her in disgust. "Well you'd better run faster!"

Ollie stepped outside and we followed him, in a stunned shock. Standing outside our house, we breathed in the smell of smoke and listened to the sound of madness and chaos unfolding around us.

"The world really is cracking up, kids," my Dad said, quite sadly. "And what is sad is that it was us that caused the cracks."

We stood there for ages, watching the smoke billowing in the sky, creating an eerie glow around us and, crazily, I felt closer to both of them in those moments than I have in years.

## Comments

**JesseBelle:** It's crazy. Just crazy. So many shops have been smashed up.

Steve was out there looting, reckoned he wanted a new TV but just came back with some sweets and some T Shirts that were too small for him

**MaisyM:** He's an idiot

**Popsicle:** I'm scared. Dad' s Merc was smashed up, he's dead mad.

I hate this. When will it end? They say there will be more.

**Boyz4Change:** This is the start! Authorities try and stop us, but we will rise!! Yeah!!

**007:** All idiots, you don't make changes by smashing up property and scaring people. Crazy.

I hope you are all safe.

## Tuesday 9th August 2011

### The Morning After….

The next morning I decided to get up early and investigate the damage. I guess I have that kind of morbid fascination deep inside of me that is hard to suppress; it's probably come from years of living on the edges of depravity.

Mum called, upset because Sweaty Keith's bike was torched during the riots. She is also upset that she wasn't caught on camera.

"I had my best dress on, low cut and everything and walked down all the main streets where the action was….and not one bloody shot!"

"You're lucky you weren't shot at!" I told her

"All I want is some recognition sweetie. I was once told I have a face for film."

The news was full of it and Dad was still ranting about a "loss of morals" and "no sense of bleedin' purpose." This was coming from a man with his head stuffed halfway down a cornflakes packet because he couldn't be bothered to wash up a bowl, or get off his bottom and go down to the shop for some milk. Small flecks of orange cereal were dotted around his grey bristle. He didn't look like someone who should be casting judgement on others.

Ollie was flopped out on the sofa opposite him, looking exhausted and texting on his phone.

"It's your lot that caused this," my Dad said, wagging a nicotine stained finger at him. "You bankers, gambling with our money."

"My lot?" Ollie shot back. "We were keeping this country afloat. Anyway, I'm not part of 'that lot' anymore."

I called Poppy up to see if she fancied coming out (to be honest I wanted the company, as I was a bit nervous in case some of the nutters were still out there). But she wasn't interested.

"I'm working on my novel today, hun." She informed me. "Besides, Dad's been bit on edge, since his car was smashed up. He's told me I have to stay in until things calm down a bit."

To say Mr Summers was a little over-protective was the understatement of the year, but I let this one go. Perhaps I was just jealous. I doubt my dad would notice where I was one day to the next, just as long as his clothes got washed and something that resembled food was served up to him each evening.

Jess on the other hand was only too happy to tag along. She only had her Mum, Stella, to worry about her, and she was hardly the maternal type. Jess said she was busy on some fundraising campaign for lesbians with no legs, or something similar.

"I told you Steve was out last night," Jess told me, a rush of excitement in her voice. "He told me it was proper mental. He smashed a window in and everything!"

Steve is really starting to bug me. I'm secretly hoping that they are not together for long. Steve is the type of guy that still thinks burps are funny.

We walked into town and barely spoke to each other. It was really eerie being in the streets, you could still smell smoke in the air and there was a weird silence hanging around us, as if the whole city was waking up in shock. Lots of people were out trying to clean up the mess with a steely resolve that was quite unnerving. A few shot us suspicious looks.

"We weren't involved, love." Jess spat at one particular scowling woman. "I was at home watching someone else's misery on Eastenders."

"And I was quaffing wine at a dinner party with Hugo over at the Manor House!" I added in what I thought would pass for a posh voice, but I don't think that helped. The woman in question shook her broom at us in a dismissive way and hissed something about "the youth of today."

I didn't take much notice to be honest. She was wearing a dodgy peach twin-set and probably only read the Daily Mail – therefore I deduced it wasn't her fault that her mind had been narrowed to the width of a pencil.

We continued walking, stepping over the broken glass and rubbish that was strewn everywhere.

"This is so freaky," Jess kept on saying. "It's like being in a bloody war zone or something."

As we moved nearer to town, we saw larger groups of people cleaning up, wielding brooms and black bags. Most of them were young. One guy with floppy red hair waved us over.

"Hey, guys – you fancy helping the cleanup effort?"

Jess looked at me and shrugged.

"Yeah, okay," I replied, thinking of the snotty cow earlier. "I'm sure we can help."

It was hard work, but it was fun. We had a laugh with the small group we worked with.

We came across a smashed-up clothes shop. I think it used to be some kind of ropey ladies boutique. Hanging out of the shattered window was a mannequin, looking a little disorientated. A great big tear across her stomach was exposing her innards and if it was at all possible to feel sorry for an inanimate object, I felt it. Her face, although displaying a rather haughty expression, seemed dismayed at being exposed in such a manner. To make matters worse she had been stripped bare.

We noticed a policeman was cleaning up the mess, looking tired and grumpy. He pulled the mannequin free from her predicament and dumped her unceremoniously on the street, arse in the air.

"Excuse me; is that going to be chucked away?" I asked

"Yeah…" he replied absently. "Take the bloody thing if you want it. Saves me having to clear it out."

So that's how Britney (well – it suited her) came to be sitting in my bedroom, decorated in my necklaces and scarves, with an old JLS T-shirt disguising her wound.

Christ knows what we looked like lugging her home, I'm sure a few curtains twitched. My Dad certainly wasn't impressed as I passed him on the stairs.

"Watch out, you nearly had my eye out there!" he yelled jabbing an accusing finger at Britney's rather pointy right digit. "What the hell is that anyway?"

"She's Britney. And she is staying!"

"Ask her if she'll pay some sodding rent then…" he muttered, before stomping off to the Pride.

And as I write this now, Britney is standing gracefully, still pointing at me (I like to think she is urging me on)

To be honest she is probably the only sane individual in this house.


### Comments

**007:** Britney? After Britney Spears?

It's pretty bleak at my end of town too. My favourite chippie was smashed up

**MasiyM:** Yeah, my Mum loves her. And the dummy looks a bit like her (Britney not my Mum)

I hate it though, it's like living in a war zone. I can still smell smoke. I'm so paranoid that Dad has set fire to his trousers.

**007:** It's not nice

I've been involved in the clean-up operation too. Quite a big one that's been organised on-line. Showing everyone that 'the youth ain't that bad' you can get involved too? If you're handy with a broom? I can send you the link?

**MaisyM:** Cool, okay, why not. I'm sure I could get a few of us together.

**007:** Cool – check out @londonriotcleanup on Twitter

**Friday 12th August 2011**

**Clean up Day**

It's amazing how quickly I got swept up into all of this. First, I thought I'd just take a little peek at @londonriotcleanup on Twitter, next I found I was following them, along with thousands of others. All keen to restore London, Manchester and other cities back to their former glory.

I also looked for a user '007' but failed to find one. I wonder who my commenter is? Certainly none of the followers that I trawled through on the website were familiar to me. Knowing my luck, he's some fat old bloke in a bedsit, munching on a kebab whilst he sends me cheerful messages.

Sorry '007' I know you will probably read this – but you can't blame a girl for wondering.

Anyway, today was a day when it was decided that a large group of us would go back out and help clean up some of the streets in South London. I managed to encourage Jess to come too. Poppy couldn't come as her Dad was still being ultra paranoid and keeping her indoors.

"I don't mind, really," she told me. "My book, Miss Stake, is coming along really well. I'd rather keep on with that."

Jess needed a little persuading but decided in the end that it might be a good day out.

My Dad was actually quite encouraging when I told him my plans. He kissed me on the cheek on his way out to the Pride.

"Sometimes you have to rise above the rats," he whispered, before skulking off to the pub.

I do wonder about him sometimes. He seems so sad at times, so full of regret. Yet on other days he acts as if he couldn't care less about anything. I miss my old Dad – the one that used to go to work in his uniform, came home and kicked his shoes off in front of the news. The Dad that only went to the Pride on Saturdays or for special occasions. Where did he go? What happened to him?

Us – that's what's happened to him.

"Where the hell are you off to?" asked Ollie, watching me emerge from the dark store cupboard, with our decrepit broom in one hand, and a fist full of bin bags in the other.

"I'm out to clean the streets," I muttered, trying to steer past an excitable Dave who seemed to think that the rather hairy broom was another dog.

Ollie sniggered and returned to his paper. I noticed that there was a package next to him, it looked suspiciously soft and teddy bear sized.

"Do you want me to post that while I'm out?" I asked, trying to catch sight of the name on the packaging.

He looked up and quickly pushed the parcel on his lap. "Nah, it's all right, I'll do it later. It's not important.... Just old crap."

At that moment Jess burst in. She was wearing the shortest skirt ever and was holding a bright pink broom that must have come from her Mum's Salon.

"Ollie!" she gushed. "Are you coming too? It's going to be a right laugh."

Ollie looked up and grinned.

"Well...I wasn't going to..."

"Oh, go on, we could do with some muscle."

I was inwardly groaning, praying that he would refuse, but of course he didn't. He told us to 'wait' while he changed his top and then ran upstairs like an excited child.

The one thing that he did do though was leave the package on the table, so I could risk a quick peek. The name on the label was 'B. Robinson'

Who the hell was B Robinson? It certainly wasn't Lottie...

It was a bit of a weird day really, walking up and down streets in the warm sunshine, surrounded by people armed with dustpans, gloves and brooms – singing and chanting. All united in one cause. It was all mainly organised by this guy called Glen, who arranged it all on Twitter. I actually got to meet him once we arrived; he was giving out disposal gloves outside the train station. He had a big, beaming face and longish, blonde hair. He reminded me a bit of a surfer.

"Thanks for coming guys," he boomed, before pointing us towards an assigned area.

At one point Nanna texted me (yes, she does have a phone, and a better one than me)

*I heard from your Mum that you're out cleaning the streets today Maisy, good for you! I'm planning to travel over to Clapham tomorrow to help with their efforts.*

I was glad that I had made her proud and I was glad that I had done something good today.

But I couldn't help but be distracted by Ollie.

Not only by the mystery parcel.

But also by the fact that he spent the whole day glued to Jess's side – laughing and joking.

They looked like a happy couple.

And that is not a good thing.


## Comments

**Glen @ LondonRiotcleanup:** Thanks for coming today Maisy, appreciated. Keep following us on Twitter. Keep up the good work!

P.S love the description – but I can't swim!

**MaisyM:** Will do – thanks for organising it! Perhaps it's about time you learnt (never too old!)

**007:** OY! I'm not sure I like my description so much. I'm not old and fat, although I do like kebabs...

I'm glad you got involved, was a great day

**MaisyM:** You were there?

**007:** Of course.

**MaisyM:** Who are you?

**007:** 007 – man of mystery!! Maybe you'll find out one day.

**MaisyM:** Really? I'm even more intrigued now (unless you are a really fat man munching kebabs!)

**007:** No – I promise I'm not ;o)

**JesseBelle:** Never mind them – you are paranoid! There is nothing going on with me and Ollie, we're just mates! You have to let this go, otherwise I will end up mad at you and I don't want that.

**MaisyM:** I don't want to upset you, I'm just warning you about him

**JesseBelle:** I'm a big girl and for your info we are meeting up this weekend. Blog about that!

**MaisyM:** Just mates and meeting up this weekend? You're 17, he's too old and too sleezy for you.

**JesseBelle:** Grow up Maisy. I'm signing off now. I don't want to read this blog any more. You're not being fair.


## Monday 15th August 2011

### The Raid

I was out at the local shops this morning, buying milk because ours had gone off AGAIN, when I got the call from my Dad.

"Maisy. Get your yourself home now.....OW, OW, MY BLEEDIN' EYES!"

Before I could ask what had happened the phone went dead. To be honest I wasn't unduly alarmed. My dad has called me once before because he lost the remote control, and another time because he couldn't work the toaster. The chances were it wasn't life threatening.

However my opinion soon changed when I rounded the corner of our road and saw the state of our house. What had been our front door was now hanging off by the hinges. My stomach twisted – what had the daft idiot done now?

Doris, the elderly deaf woman next door, was standing by her garden gate, fingering her roses, obviously waiting for someone to come along so that she could offload her gossip.

"You've been raided!" She shouted at me proudly, sucking in her bottom lip like they do when they haven't got any teeth.

"What do you mean, raided?" I shouted back, feeling a bit rude. But what else can you do when they refuse to wear a hearing aid?

"What do you think I mean? R A I D E D," she said slowly, like I was mental. "Reckon they thought you were involved in the riots. Reckon you were seen with some stolen goods...."

"What stolen goods?" I was booming now, my frustration growing.

I looked at her eyes; they were gleaming with malevolent joy. Suddenly the penny dropped, she had seen me with Britney. She had assumed I had stolen her.

"You stupid cow," I muttered. "A policeman gave me that mannequin, I didn't take her!" I barged past her and raced into the house which was strangely silent. I found Dad slumped in his chair in his pants, rubbing his eyes.

"Maisy?" He croaked. "About time. Those police stormed in here, said they had reports you had been rioting."

"I wasn't."

"I know that! You were here with me. But some know-it-all saw you carry that doll home and shopped you in." He peered up at me, his eyes were watering. "The thing is they burst in unannounced, they might have knocked but I was asleep so I heard nothing…..anyway the bloody dog started barking and going crazy so they squirted him with some kind of evil deodorant!"

"Oh, my god, poor Dave. Is he OK? Where is he?"

"Sod the dog, he took off. What about me?" My Dad was standing up now flapping at his eyes in a dramatic fashion. "That stuff has got right into my face. Here I am a man in his own house, sleeping off a little drink and then this craziness erupts! Given me a right shock. I'm practically an old man, you know! Why do that to decent folk?"

I'm not sure that a man in his sixties unconscious in his pants and stinking of booze could ever be referred to as decent….

"Did they take Britney?" I asked him

"Nah. They just wanted to see if you had been nicking stuff. When they saw all you had was that useless dummy, they buggered off again with barely an apology. Now I've got to get onto the Council about that front door. Any maniac could get in…"

I gave Dad a cold flannel and left him grumbling in his chair. Luckily an episode of Countdown was on to cheer him up (he feels achievement in finding four letter words; "look Maz 'FISH', none of those so-called-experts saw FISH."

My concerns at the moment are mainly with Dave, who seems to have vanished into thin air. I've worn my feet out, going up and down knocking on the houses in the neighbouring streets. And I've rung up the dog wardens in the area and three animal rescue centres.

"I don't know why you care," Dad said unhelpfully. "I'm glad to see the back of his stinky bum. With any luck some Chinese fella will stick him in a kebab."

This only goes to prove that my dad's knowledge of cuisine or culture is not the best.

I even called the police in a rage but apparently mistakes happen and in "these difficult times" more desperate and immediate measures are required. I am still fuming with deaf Doris, though, and vow to train Dave to wee on her precious roses as soon as he returns.

## Comments

**Glen @ LondonRiotCleanup:** You're kidding? The police just burst in? Man, that's harsh, hope you're ok babe.

**MaisyM:** Thanks, just want my dog back.

**Lucy Locket:** Poor you. I hope he comes back soon. I'll keep everything crossed

**MaisyM:** Thank you

**007:** Aw no, that's awful. I can't believe they raided your home for a shop dummy! Is your Dad alright? I hope Dave comes back quickly.

**MasiyM:** Thank you. Dad is fine, but his eyes are a bit bloodshot. Ollie has taken him to the Pride to recover.

**007:** Don't panic, dogs are very intelligent; he'll find his way back to you.

**MaisyM:** I hope you're right.

## Wednesday 17th August 2011

## Desperately Seeking Dave

I'm missing Dave….

I miss his smell.

I miss his bark.

I even miss stepping in his poo…

I'm too sad to blog. I never thought I would miss the smelly mutt as much as I do.

I just want my dog back.

## Comments

**Lucy Locket:** Sending you cyber hugs. I hope you feel better soon

**Glen @LondonRiotCleanup:** Hey! Don't be sad. It's not over yet. I'll put stuff out on Twitter and on our website. Dave won't be lost for long.

**MaisyM:** You're so kind Glen

**007:** I'll keep my eyes peeled too, bit further out from you I think. But you never know...

### Friday 19th August 2011

### Yes! Yes! Yes!

You know what; I really thought Dave was a goner. I actually had a dream where a rich family adopted him, a bit like Oliver Twist, and he ended up living in a big house with a clean bum and a fresh bone to chew on every day.

Poppy and Jess have been amazing, they have come out with me walking the streets, looking for the lanky mutt of no particular breed. Even Ollie has stuck up a few posters and knocked on a couple of doors. The hand drawn picture of Dave wasn't that great though (I'm not very good at Art). Dad said it looked like a short-legged goat with a prolapsed uterus.

"He'll come back, sis," Ollie said softly when he came back from his last efforts, but he didn't sound convincing,

It's even worse when you are trying to describe him to the welfare charities on the phone:

"Yeah he's medium size, sort of brown and lanky with floppy ears and a drippy bottom. He likes eating butter and my Dad's socks. Does that help?"

Just when I had started to give up I got a call on my mobile. Someone had seen Glen's message on Twitter (which had been re-tweeted thousands of times, how amazing is that!) The chap said. "Please come and get him as I've been cleaning up dog poo constantly for days now!"

That certainly sounded like my dog.

Poppy agreed to come with me, just in case the man was a mass murderer or something. She was at a loose end anyway as she was experiencing writer's block.

Luckily the guy only lived a short tram ride away.

"I have Violet meeting the rogue vampire, but I have no idea how to encourage their first romantic encounter," she explained in a state of near despair. I seriously think she needs to get out more. She's not even watching TV as much at the moment, and that in itself is a concern.

I was unable to help with her current problem as romance is not a subject I'm greatly familiar with. My only boyfriends have been Eddie (I was thirteen and more awkward than I am now, we used to snog behind the shops and that was about it) and Callum who was more recent, but who is not worth writing about. Besides, Melissa Henderson has her claws in him now.

All the way to collecting my dog, Poppy was rabbiting on about the need to "expand her character" and "fulfil the needs of the protagonist" or some such rubbish. I started to switch off and think about my new job next week. I know it's only a temporary thing, but I'm already getting stressed out.

I've never worked before.

I don't think Saturday jobs count. I didn't really do much; just got shoes out of a box, showed them to the customer and put them through the till. Sometimes I might even speak, if I could be arsed. Saturday jobs are just a filler, you don't learn anything – most of the time you leave your brain at home, still sleeping cosily in bed.

I started worrying because Dan, Dan the Recruitment Man had called me this morning to check I was all set to go. He has a nice manner on the phone; I can see why he's in sales, all bright and breezy – even on a dark, dank morning.

"I've lost my dog," I told him straight away. I'm not sure why.

"Oh, I'm sorry," he said, and he sounded sincere. "That's awful. I hope you find him soon."

"Me too. I miss the smelly, old thing."

He laughed and it reminded me of some actor I had seen once on TV, with one of those big hearty laughs. Not the dirty snigger my Dad's got, or the girly giggle that Ollie has.

He wished me luck for tomorrow and that's when I started to feel nervous. God! I wish he hadn't called now!

Luckily the chap that had found Dave lived only a few roads away from the tram stop, so I didn't have too long to think, but it could have been miles away the difference it made – eerily my dream had almost come true, for although not a mansion, this house was far grander and nicer than ours.

The guy in the house was very tall and fairly broad with one of those large jolly faces that look as if they are laughing all the time. He reminded me of a game show host. I expected him to produce Dave on a silver platter and declare:

"Just look at what you've won!"

But instead, Dave padded meekly out of another room and eyed us both suspiciously.

"He has been as good as gold," the guy told me. "But I have to say, he does seem to have a problem in his rectal region. You might want to get that checked out."

I thanked him (choosing to ignore his last comment) and left him and Poppy chatting while I walked over to give Dave lots of well-deserved affection and a bit of a telling-off for not coming home.

I was quite pleased to leave the man's house though, if I'm honest. The place had a strange smell, a bit yeasty. And he had clammy hands. Nanna told me never to trust a man with clammy hands.

Once I was home, Dave ran in, obviously relieved to see normality resumed and the sound of the TV blaring once again. He trotted into the kitchen and found a dirty sock by the washing machine to nibble.

Even Olllie gave him an affectionate ruffle of the fur.

"He's not so bad," he mumbled. "Once you get to know him."

And then he looked up at me and winked.


## Comments

**Lucy Locket:** Yeah! He's home. So pleased for you.

**Glen @LondonRiotCleanup:** Fantastic, so glad the tweet worked. Nothing like the power of the internet! Give me a shout if you need help with anything else

**007:** I'm so pleased Dave is back, means I can stop trawling my local streets shouting his name like a lunatic ;o)

Hope you are smiling again

**MaisyM:** I am, I really am!


**Saturday 20th August 2011**

**Hair Dye Disaster**

It was one of Mums gigs this evening and I promised her that I would go. She wanted Ollie to come too, but he shrugged and said he 'had plans' and then started texting with a nasty smile on his face.

Poppy agreed to come with me but Jess couldn't make it, she was seeing Steve. I think he wanted to boast about his rioting exploits.

I went to Poppy's house first, as she had agreed to dye my hair. I have decided that I am sick of my mousey non-colour, and want to be a brunette. I was a bit scared to do it by myself, so I was hoping another pair of eyes (and hands) would make the process a little easier.

I love being at Poppy's house. It's always a bit surreal. Most of the rooms are pink and flouncy. There are cushions everywhere. It must be what it's like to be inside a giant marshmallow. There is no trace of her Dad, apart from his small study, which is grey, gloomy and stinks of smoke. A bit like the big man himself.

Poppy's Mum, Linda, is also very frilly and fancy, so she has obviously designed the house to suit her personality. She always wears pastel shades, has finely groomed hair and never goes out without her make-up on.

The bookshelves are full of the romantic literature that Poppy and Linda devour, and there are cabinets full of videos and DVDs, mainly of the naffest films you could ever imagine, most of which never got anywhere near a cinema.

What I love most about Poppy's house is the towers of CDs in her dining room, all bought from some weird and wacky company that Linda had subscribed to after watching a dubious five minute advertisement on cable TV. The CDs all have a love theme, and include:

Love songs to grind to

Love songs to woo to

Love songs to reminisce to

And even

Love songs to die to (how romantic...)

I made Poppy play 'Love songs to dine to' while she washed the dye out of my hair. There's nothing like having a strange man warbling on about leaving his 'cake out in the rain' while your mate is hosing your hair down.

"Why did he leave a cake out in the rain anyway?" I asked above the noise of the shower. "Bloody stupid thing to do if you ask me. What did he expect to happen? It was hardly going to enhance the flavour!"

"It's one of my Mum's favourite songs," Poppy said, all seriously. "And apparently it has a hidden sexual subtext."

"Eh?"

"Oh, I dunno. It's probably just him wanting a shag or something…."

Poppy was starting to dry my hair quite roughly. I heard her take a sharp intake of breath and immediately began to panic.

"What's wrong? Has it come out red or something?"

"No, no. The colour is fine."

Poppy then fled the room shouting, "Wait there!"

I sat there, not daring to move, dripping all over the floor. Not only that but the song had changed and some other bloke was shouting about the 'world being a great big onion'.

I was starting to feel a little sick…

Poppy returned clutching a bottle of nail vanish remover. She had a sheepish look on her face. I was not feeling reassured.

"Now, I don't want you to worry…" she started – and my stomach immediately did a double backflip. "But I've got a little tiny bit of hair dye on your forehead!"

"What?" I leaped up and dared to look in the mirror. It was bad. All across my hairline, ears and even on the end of my nose were large brownish stains. I looked like a freak.

"How did you manage that?" I shrieked. "Are you blind? My Dad would have made a better job half cut!"

"It's OK" she said, in the silly soothing voice she has. "This'll work."

I can assure you that having your skin viciously wiped with nail varnish remover and cotton wool, is about as unpleasant as it gets. The dye stains were removed, but I was left with great red rashes from all the rubbing. I'm sure I've lost a layer of skin.

Although I had to confess the hair colour itself looked OK, we both ended up giggling over it.

"I wish Jess had seen this, you rubbing nail polish remover into my head – she would have taken the right mick!" I joked.

I felt sad then. I had not really seen much of Jess in the last few days. Poppy patted my hand as if she knew.

"You know, it'll work out in the end," she soothed.

"What will?"

"The three of you. You, her and Ollie?"

"Eh?"

Poppy looked surprised. "Didn't you know that's who she's with tonight?"

"No." I felt a little bit sick, remembering Ollie's cruel smile earlier. "She told me she was seeing Steve."

Poppy sighed. "I don't think she's with him anymore. You heard he's been arrested for looting? Jess isn't very impressed. I'm sorry. I thought you knew."

We left the house a little subdued. I thought about texting Jess, but then thought better of it. What was the point? She's made her decision. Now I've just got to watch and wait while Ollie breaks another girl's heart.

And as for Mum's gig, what a total waste of time. We arrived to see them perform two songs, before they were booed off.

To be fair the crowd were mainly our age (or suspiciously younger) and Mum was trying to entice them with a Bananarama song. It was just never going to work.

We slipped out before we were seen. I didn't want Mum to know I had seen her do so badly.

Or perhaps I didn't want her to see that I was embarrassed. I'm not really sure…

I really don't think I like my family that much.

*Comments*

**Lucy Locket:** No-one likes their family that much hun. Don't stress.

Let your friend chose her own path.

**007:** Keep smiling. No-one chooses their family, their chosen for you.

You should meet my Mum – she'd make yours seem practically saintly.

**MaisyM:** Really? Is she that bad?

**007:** If I told you, you probably wouldn't believe me. The word neurotic was invented for her!


## Sunday 21st August 2011

### Kev Kirby Cocks Up

Nanna was so excited about this evening with Kev Kirby that she has been phoning me all week to make sure I hadn't forgotten.

"I know what you're like Maisy, you've got the memory of a gerbil!"

This is coming from the woman who, two minutes later, left me hanging on the phone while she went to answer the door – and promptly forgot that I was there. I had to call back three hours later when the silly cow had finally put her phone back on the hook.

I agreed to meet her outside the church at 7pm. I didn't bother getting dressed up, it's not exactly a night out. I just fed the men their fish fingers and Dave his usual cheap dog food (which he sniffed at reluctantly and then slowly began to eat). To be fair, his bum has improved. I've only had to clear up one mess this week – and that was after Dad had too many cans, tripped over the sleeping dog and screamed 'bastard' at the top of his lungs. I think he pooed outside Dad's room out of spite.

Nanna was on time for once and waiting outside the Spiritualist Church - which actually doesn't look like a church at all; it just looks like another house in a line of dull terraced buildings. The only thing to distinguish it was a small sign above the red door indicating its purpose, and a smaller notice under it, politely asking us to wipe our feet.

"You made it, then!" Nanna barked at me.

She was dressed very formally in her best blue coat and hat, and was carrying her umbrella, even though it was a clear night.

"Is that little slime-ball still at your place?" she asked, pointing her brolly at me quite aggressively,

"Which one?"

She laughed. "Good point. Well I've accepted that your father isn't going anywhere. I meant your brother. Is he still sitting around on his arse feeling sorry for himself?"

I told her he was. I told her that he had barely moved from the sofa, apart from making a few angry calls to Lottie. He wasn't talking about his next plans now and seemed quite content to watch the rubbish on TV with Dad.

"Bloody men." Nanna muttered as we walked into the church. "You wait until I come over; I'll give them what for."

I didn't doubt it.

Inside the church was a small, hall-like space packed full of chairs, lined up to face a stage. There was already a fair few people there. I could tell that Nanna was getting excited, she kept adjusting her hat and skirt as if she was about to meet someone incredibly important.

"He's meant to be good, this Kev Kirby," she whispered at me, spittle flying into my ear. "Pru Jennings saw him last year and he made contact with her horse! Her horse, would you believe?"

"But horses don't talk!"

"They can still communicate. It's all spirit, isn't it!"

Nanna guided us to the front. She needed to be there as she is pretty deaf, but she refuses to wear a hearing aid as she says they are for 'old people.' Nanna is seventy-five next birthday.

The evening started with singing, which I found particularly hard, especially as I was made to sit next to a man with huge thighs, who sang 'Angels' in a very deep, baritone voice. This was in comparison to my Nanna who can't sing for toffee and was going up and down more times than an excitable bungee jumper.

I was relieved when the agony of the joyful singing was over (apparently done to bring the spirits into the room, personally I think it would have driven them away, screaming). Nanna started to jiggle up and down next to me. At first (remembering the amount of Tena Ladies I've seen in her toilet), I thought she needed a wee, but then I realised that Kev Kirby had just walked onto the stage.

He had his eyes shut and he was humming, which was a bit odd. His long hair was swept away from his face, but to me he still looked like a dodgy rock singer. I expected him to whip out a guitar and start head-banging. Instead he raised his long arms in the air. I could see small sweat patches already forming under his arms.

"I can feel the spirits are with me," he said softly.

I felt the bloke next to me stiffen in anticipation. The whole room seemed to be hanging on his every word.

"I can feel a connection with a woman," he said. "An older woman. Has anyone here had an older woman pass over to the over side?"

There was a stir in the crowd, mutterings. I was starting to feel uncomfortable. Most of the people in the room were over fifty, so there was a good chance that they would have lost a mother or grandmother – it was hardly rocket science.

As I expected, several hands went up.

"I can see her now," Kev continued, waving his hands in the air. "She is old and wise. A mother perhaps? She had white hair."

"That's my Mum!" screamed some woman in the third row, jumping up. She was wearing a bright pink tracksuit and was clutching a small doll. "That's my Mum, Rose, I just know it."

"Now, don't tell me anything else," the man said smoothly. "But was she named after a flower?"

"Yes, yes. Rose! I knew it was her!"

"And, I have a feeling she gave you that very doll you're holding today?" he asked.

"Yes, yes she did." The woman was crying now. Although why I wasn't sure, she was hardly being fed new information.

"Your mother is saying she is at peace now and she loves you very much…"

"Oh thank you!" More tears.

This was complete rubbish.

I spent the rest of the hour, sitting in a trance-like state watching while this Kev Kirby came up with loose descriptions and connected them to desperate members of the audience. I felt myself drifting off, wishing I had gone down the Pride instead with Jess and Poppy. Jess was bound to be telling Poppy all about her date with Ollie and what they had got up to. Interestingly I hadn't seen my brother all day. Maybe they had had a row and she'd sent him packing back to London? Here's hoping...

My full attention wasn't grabbed again until he said.

"I have a man here and I think he's connected to you!"

And he pointed at my Nanna.

Nanna nearly shot out of her seat with shock.

"Is it my Johnny?" she asked softly.

"Yes, he tells me his name is Johnny!" Kev Kirby confirmed helpfully. "He says he misses you and that his passing was peaceful."

Nanna nodded, no emotion (that's not her style) but satisfied.

But Kev wasn't finished.

"I can also see that he was a kind, caring man and that you had a very loving relationship."

"Eh?" My Nanna said.

"You had a beautiful, loving relationship," Kev repeated calmly (and slightly louder and slower, just in case my Nanna was both deaf and stupid).

At this point she got up, adjusted her hat and then grabbed my hand.

"Come on Maisy," she said, very loudly. "We're going. This is farcical."

Then she turned to Kev Kirby and said. "For your information Mr Kirby, my husband was and always was a miserable old sod and we had a loveless, sexless relationship. I miss him but God knows why. You are either talking to the wrong Johnny up there, or you are talking out of your bum-hole."

And with that we both left the building.

I think my Nanna might be taking a break from Spiritualism for a bit.

## Comments

**Lucy Locket:** How funny, I wish I could have seen his face.

**007:** You wondered who I am? I am actually Kev Kirby and I'm very upset. It took me ages to connect with those damn spirits.

**MaisyM:** Please tell me you're not

**007:** Nah. I'm not sure I could do all that touchy-feely stuff. Good on your Nanna. She is a top girl

**Popiscle:** I knew I should have come. The Pride was OK, but we missed you.

**MaisyM:** Did Jess talk about Ollie

**Popiscle:** A bit. They had fun. She says he's a nice guy.

**MaisyM:** Xo(

## Monday 22nd August 2011

### First Day

I can't lie. I was getting even more nervous about my first day at work as the day grew closer, even though it's only a temp job. Christ knows what I would be like if I ever got something permanent.

The trouble is, nerves always have the same effect on me – and meant that I was stuck on the loo for twenty minutes with a dodgy tummy. This did not please Dad, who stood outside hammering on the door, complaining about his "sixty year old bladder." Honestly, he is a fine one to talk. Dad would happily spend an hour "in his office," Viz comic in his hand, "brewing his poo." It is his long held belief that you should "never strain, or you'll burst a vein." He told Granddad that after his first stroke. I don't think he appreciated it much.

"Some things should never be rushed, Maz," he says with relish.

Well, today it felt like my whole body was in a rush. It was as if my system was in overdrive and everything was spilling over. Even my nose was starting to run. I must have looked a right state. I just hope I looked smart enough in my only suit, which is cheap polyester and makes that funny noise if you move too fast.

I didn't have enough money for the bus, so I had to walk very briskly, hoping that I wouldn't develop sweat patches on the way.

MJ Design is on the outskirts of town and is a very small, dark looking building with tiny windows and a funny mono-pitched roof. The J on the sign was also wonky and, worryingly, looked like it could fall on someone's head at any moment.

I walked straight into the main office as there was no reception to speak of. There was a group of what I assumed were designers on one side of the room and on the other a small, very nervous looking girl. She looked younger than me. When I came in, she beckoned me over.

"You must be the temp," she said softly, her breath stunk of mints and her eyes were darting all over the place. "I'm Becca. The manager, Sheila, will be out shortly."

She gestured to a side office where I assumed Sheila was hiding. She looked terrified.

I wasn't really sure what I was meant to do while I was waiting, so I popped myself down at the vacant desk beside Becca. A small computer was in front with a screensaver flashing up "keep calm, and carry on." I could feel my stomach gurgling and started to worry where the toilets were.

Sheila seemed to take forever to come out of her dark side office and I felt so daft just sitting there staring at my torn up nails, trying to look relaxed and happy. When the door finally opened I nearly leapt out of my seat in anticipation.

Sheila wasn't what I had been expecting, while I had been sitting there allowing myself to daydream. She was very small and very skinny, with a plain, pinched face and short, tightly curled blonde hair. There was a permanent crease between her eyes that made her look extremely annoyed.

Actually, she *was* annoyed.

"So you're the temp!" she said without a hint of joy. "I'm Sheila. I'm your boss. I'm not going to bother with inductions as you are only going to be here for five minutes, but I *will* tell you that the fire exit is over there!"

She pointed vaguely at a door in the opposite corner. Several boxes were piled in front of it. I'm no expert but I'm sure that's not legal. How the hell would I be able to clamber over that lot if the place was ablaze?

"You're here because we are having an audit done next week and everything needs to be squeaky clean. Therefore there is a lot of shredding and filing to do…"

"Ok," I replied.

"I hope you like the mundane? I hope you relish the boring?"

"Yes of course." I whispered back. What else was I meant to say? No, this sounds awful? And why are you talking to me like I'm the scum of the Earth?

She looked at me with complete and utter contempt and then ordered me to make the tea. Not normal bloody tea either. Earl bloody Grey. Who drinks that except the Queen? Or an Earl?

And so that was my first day. Shredding ream after ream of paper. I'm not even sure why I was shredding some of it, as a lot had "urgent" stamped across the top in bright red letters. But my job was not to ask questions, mine was simply to follow orders like a brain-dead sheep.

Even worse was the filing, there was heaps of it, in no particular order. It all needs to be sorted and stored away in these ancient cabinets that look like they haven't seen the light of day for years.

For the rest of my shift, every time I caught Sheila's eye, a small scowl would form and her lip would curl ever-so slightly. I could imagine a forked tongue slipping out from her tightly clenched mouth and lashing towards me.

Put it this way – I get the distinct impression that she doesn't like me. Or anything that breathes for that matter…

## Comments

**Lucy Locket:** Keep at it hun, I'm sure it'll improve. At least it's some experience for your CV.

I got the waitressing job but its minimum wage. I hope I get some office work soon.

**MaisyM:** Thanks. I hope you find something good soon too

**Glen @LondonRiotCleanup:** Blocked fire exits! Shredding urgent docs. Hmm, this sounds dodgy. I assume you are using a fake company name on this blog, but perhaps you should report these cowboys. Job or no job?

**MaisyM:** Yes, fake name. Not sure I have enough to report just yet…

**007:** I would speak to your agent.

But as Lucy said, at least it's good for your CV

## Wednesday 24th August 2011

### Texting

Another rubbish day at work. I won't even bother blogging about it. I don't think I have the energy.

I'm sure Sheila isn't human though, she's like something from one of Poppy's vampire films. She certainly drains the life out of everyone around her.

Anyway, when I got home I felt sad and restless so I decided to text Jess. It went something like this:

Me: Hi babe. Not seen u in ages. U ok?

Jess: Yeah. All cool. U?

Me: Job sucks.

Jess: Stick at it babe. Mite improve

Me: How's Steve

Jess: Dunno. Think he's been done for lootin. Not seen him

Me: Why?

Jess: I'm bored of him. Need a break.

Me: What about Ollie?

Jess: Maybe. See how it goes. Does that bother you?

Me: I guess. But I want you to be happy

Jess: Then leave it alone. And stop being so hard on him.

Me: Ok...I'll try 4 U

Jess: Thank U xx


### Comments

**Lucy Locket:** Aw I think you did the right thing

**Popiscle:** Me too xx

**Thursday 25th August 2011**

**And so it continues....**

I'm hoping work gets better, but my time here is not improving. Sheila is so hard to work for, or even to like. She's like a nightmare headmistress crossed with a deranged dragon with toothache.

The first annoying thing is that I have to ask permission every time I want to go the toilet. And the look of disgust I get when I ask is pretty unnecessary if you ask me. After all, everyone's bladder needs emptying once in a while; it's a basic, bodily function. I managed to find the loo okay. A poky little room with a basic toilet and washbasin, with a suspicious-looking towel hanging alongside that looked as if it was breeding more germs than our fridge at home (and that's saying something). However, as I was sitting there, pants around my ankles, scrabbling to find the end of the cheap and scratchy toilet roll, a rapping started on the door.

Assuming it was someone who urgently needed to go for a wee, I scraped uselessly at the roll (by now in shreds) and squeaked, "just a minute."

"Maisy. You have been four minutes already!" barked the bitch behind the door. "How long does it take for you to urinate? This is office time you are wasting!"

I couldn't believe she was timing me! Did she have a stopwatch out there? And under pressure, I still couldn't find an end to the bloody tissue. In the end I had to wipe myself with the few shreds I had managed to yank off. I was left feeling uncomfortably damp.

"Thanks to you I will be stinking of wee now," I whispered into the wall.

"What was that?" *Jesus!* She had the ears of a cat. "You've been five minutes now."

"I'm coming!" I snapped.

I quickly dared to splash my hands under the tap and, eyeing the stained towel again, I decided to use my un-absorbent polyester skirt to dry myself. It left a nice little damp patch.

I came out to find Sheila standing there, hands on hips. "Six minutes is far too long, Maisy. You have to learn to manage your time better, even when it comes to using the bathroom!"

I could feel my stomach shrink at the thought of such demands. I've always had been weak in that area – my bladder has always been a bit like a teabag. Christ knows what I'll be like by the time I'm an old lady (I'm judging this on Nanna and not holding out much hope).

I left work with an achy bladder, because going to the loo was too much of a stress.

And then what happens? I walk into the living room to find my Dad sitting there, with a tampon stuck up his right nostril.

"What the hell?" Was all I managed to say, my eyes glued to the dangly piece of string hanging from his nose. He looked completely nonchalant, as if having Tampax rammed up there was perfectly normal.

"We've run out of bog roll," he said simply, his eyes not moving from the TV.

"So?"

"And so, I had a nosebleed. I had to use something – so I grabbed one of your lady-thingys. It's bloody useful, too."

I really don't know what is worse – the fact that my own father was rifling through, then using my sanitary products, or the fact that he referred to them as "lady-thingys".

I left the room as quickly as I entered, feeling rather nauseous, which was made worse when I staggered upstairs and stepped into one of Dave's dirty piles. I couldn't even shout at the mutt. He probably got too excited about being back home again. I think I will need to call a vet soon though.

To make it worse, we had no bog roll to clean it up with – so in some kind of twisted revenge I used a pair of Dad's freshly boiled pants.

This really is what my life has become, scrubbing an already stained and tatty carpet with a pair of over-sized Y-fronts.

I'm only seventeen and sometimes I feel like my life is over already


## Comments

**Popiscle:** Your job sounds awful. What's wrong with the witch lady? Maybe you should start wearing nappies?

**MaisyM:** Don't joke – I might consider it

**Glen @LondonRiotCleanup:** It's a disgrace. You're allowed comfort breaks, it's a basic human right. Start timing her and see how she likes it!

**007:** I really think you should talk to your agency so they can sort it out...She sounds a bit of a nightmare.

P.S Your Dad is very inventive

**MaisyM:** That's one word for him!

Yes I will call them if things don't improve

**Lucy Locket:** Blimey, I thought rude customers were bad enough. Poor you!

## Saturday 27th August 2011

### Adam Fiddler

The last thing I expected today, after making Dad and Ollie's breakfast, was to receive a call from Adam – the guy from Sweaty Keith's party.

"Your mum gave me your number. I, um, hope you don't mind?" He said. He sounded a bit stuttery on the phone, it was quite sweet.

"No, it's fine," I said.

I was a little distracted at the time, as I was trying to scrape the remains of dried scrambled eggs into the bin. Ollie and Dad were slumped in the living room watching 'Homes Under The Hammer' on Cable.

Ollie was also busy telling Dad that he reckoned he could make it in property, "buy a clapped out house, spruce it up a bit, piece of piss."

Dad's nodding along like he knows all about it. He doesn't even own this house. Property scares Dad, he reckons it's something only 'the middle classes have.' That's rubbish because Melissa Henderson's parents own their own house, and they're about as far removed from middle class as you can get.

"I wondered if you'd like to come for a meal with me, tonight," Adam was saying, all polite. "I can get us a table at my favourite place?"

I hesitated, I have to admit. Adam was nice looking but he hadn't exactly excited me. That said, I was tempted by a decent meal and I thought I should at least give him a chance. He might be better company on a one-to-one basis.

We agreed to meet outside the Pride. I couldn't face having anyone pick me up at the house. Dad would scare even the most persistent nutcase away.

He was there when I arrived, dressed in skinny black jeans and a leather jacket. He looked OK – quite stylish – until he waved.

OK, I know a wave shouldn't put me off, but it was a big, girly enthusiastic wave – like the type Poppy does when she's over-excited. I had that horrible moment where I was thinking, "Please don't let anyone I know see me now." How bad was that? After all, I hardly looked great. I was wearing ancient jeans and a tatty jacket and probably needed a good haircut.

I knew I had to give him a proper chance.

"Thanks for meeting me, Maisy!" he gushed. "You won't regret dating Adam Fiddler."

"Fiddler?" I wanted to snigger.

"Yes, like a violin player," he replied, complete with cheesy grin.

Or like a paedophile.

My mouth remained firmly shut as we walked to his favourite Italian restaurant, because Adam Fiddler did not stop talking, mainly about his favourite sci-fi films and all about the time he met George Lucas at Gatwick Airport.

If I said he was dull that would be harsh, but my ears felt like they were being punished.

Finally, he stopped talking when we came to a tatty looking building on the outskirts of town. There was a badly drawn picture of an Italian flag on the window.

"Here we are!" he said brightly, struggling to push open the stiff door.

This was a Saturday night and the place was dead (apart from an elderly bloke in the corner, reading a paper). The inside was scruffy, old fashioned and smelt a bit damp. Adam led us to a table by the streaky window. Several dead flies were lined up on the sill.

"This is your favourite place?" I asked, trying to suppress the surprise.

"Well, it's cheap and it's near home," he replied quite frankly. I felt really appreciated.

A waiter (if you could call him that) came out from the back room. He was dressed in jeans and a stained white T-shirt. He didn't smile. He just thrust two laminated sheets of paper at us and hovered over us while we made our orders.

I tried to pick the thing least likely to give me food poisoning, deciding eventually on a plain pizza, and prayed that the kitchen was cleaner than our table, which looked grimy and chipped. I wondered if they had even heard of Environmental Health here.

The conversation changed during dinner, as I picked half-heartedly at my pizza (and I was bloody starving). Adam starting talking about his mother and how wonderful he thought she was. Apparently they had an extremely close bond.

"Dad left when I was a baby," he explained. "Mum had to do everything for me, she's an amazing woman. I have so much time for her."

I guess this made me warm to him a little, at least he was respectful. It was a shame that he was allowing the pasta sauce to dribble down his chin while he talked. I longed to wipe his chin with my napkin, but didn't think he would appreciate the gesture.

Adam also talked at length about his job in a newsagent's.

"It's not much," he admitted. "But I hope to be a manager one day."

With this he showed realistic ambition. I once knew a guy who seriously wanted to be an astronaut and would not be talked out of it. Because of his pure single-minded approach, he refused to work anyway else. I've since heard that he is still sitting in his Mums back bedroom watching Apollo 13 over and over. Sometimes ambition can be a dangerous thing.

I told Adam about my new job at MJ Design and he brightened up immediately.

"Me and my Mum live on the next road!" he said excitedly. "You'll have to come over for dinner after work next week."

So the date ended, strangely, with my agreeing to go to Adam's house to meet his 'amazing mum.' I figured it would be another free meal. And he wasn't such a bad person.

At least he had nice teeth.

Maybe he'll grow on me – like a fungus.

## Comments

**Glen @LondonRiotCleanUp:** He sounds like a great catch Maisy...Seriously, I remember you from the clean-up. You can do much better!

**MaisyM:** Thanks. He's not so bad, honestly. I'd like to give him a chance.

**Glen@Londonriotcleanup:** You're a pretty girl. Don't under-sell yourself.

**MaisyM:** I'm blushing now...

**007:** Sounds like you have an admirer Miss Malone. But I agree, this guy sounds a bit wet. You might need a mop for your next date...

**MaisyM:** Lol – don't be mean!


## Monday 29th August 2011

## Work Day Blues

## ARGHHHHHH!!!!!

That sums up today. I actually have blisters on my hands from shredding.

And that cow Sheila timed me on the loo again! I only took three minutes, is that really excessive? Am I really taking too long to wee? I'm starting to get a complex now. It's not my fault I had complicated buttons on my trousers to deal with too (that adds another minute onto matters I'm sure!) Maybe I should replace all the buttons on my clothes with Velcro?

I'm not writing anything else tonight. I'm going to flop in front of the TV and watch what I want for a change (as both Ollie and Dad are down the Pride tonight).

I will say now that there is a VERY high chance that I may not survive the week.


## Comments

**Lucy Locket:** Chin up Maisy. Keep saying to yourself its only temp and you'll soon be out

**MaisyM:** That's the only thing keeping me going. That and the dreams about stabbing Sheila in the eye with a pen

**Popiscle:** Poor you, we'll have to meet up soon for a girlie chat. I've been a bit caught up with Miss Stake, it's all so consuming, but I'm nearly there – first draft almost done. Have you heard from Jess?

**MaisyM:** No, not since my last text to her. But Ollie has been out every night this week...

**Popiscle:** Yeah, they do seem to be getting on well...


## Thursday 1st September 2011

### Kill me now!!

Do you know what? I think I'm brain dead. I think that Sheila is an alien from the 'Planet of Toilet Wardens' or 'Deranged Bog Watchers' and has been sent to Earth to completely drain me of energy.

She doesn't do much work herself, she just stands over my shoulder, tutting or shaking her evil head.

She told me my shredding technique is 'poor'. How can anyone have a poor shredding technique? All I do is feed paper into a machine. (Admittedly I did nearly garrotte myself with my necklace once when I leant in too close.)

I can only take my loo breaks when she pops out, otherwise I will be timed. Although, annoyingly, I notice she has numerous fag breaks and I wonder just how cost-effective they are?

I hate her. I hate her so much that I could quite happily remove her nasty tongue from her miserable face and feed that through the shredder, using my "wrong technique."

But maybe that's taking things too far?

I want to scream

Aaaargh!!

Nah. I don't feel much better.

The only positive thing I have done today is made an appointment with the vet for Dave. Hopefully this will resolve his bottom problem and stop me from having to clean up poo every morning.

If I can remove one nasty stress from my life, it would be good.

## Comments

**Glen @LondonRiotCleanUp:** I am going to come into your work and arrest this mad 'bog watcher' for crimes against bladders.

**MaisyM:** Please, can you? That would be funny

**Glen@LondonRiotCleanup:** Just send me the address and I'll be there...

## Saturday 3rd September 2011

### Supermarket Hell!

Today, I made the very unwise decision to go supermarket shopping with Dad. I made this oh-so-sensible decision because we only had a block of cheese left in the fridge and a tub of marmite in the cupboard – and also because Dad was the only one with cash (until I get paid and Ollie sorts himself out – though why he hasn't got any money left from his last job is beyond me). At least Dad has his benefit, which may be spent tonight down the Pride, so I need to catch him quick!

Dad was complaining and grumbling about going, saying that his back was hurting and what would he do if he 'needed a wee?'

"They do have public loos there, Dad!"

"Ah, but I don't like public toilets. You don't know where people have been."

This is coming from the man who avoids washing more often than a tramp.

I could only take him by agreeing to get a bus there and a lift back with Norm – who agreed to do so, as long as he got a pint later. I'm not overly happy as Norm drives a clapped-out Mini that only just scraped past its last MOT. He's also a rubbish driver. My Dad is perfectly capable of walking, but the idea fills him with dread. If we had more money he would invest in one of those mobility scooters. He watches other pensioners driving them with what can only be described as jealousy.

"One day I shall I have a chariot of my own," he says, as if it was something to aspire to.

If he ever gets one, I want to get him a personalised number plate with G1T on it.

He also made me insist that we bought faggots and peas. In fact he would only come if I promised to include them on my list. My Dad has a thing for faggots – not the proper gory ones that you see on cooking programmes that are made from pig bums or something else gross – I mean the meat based ones in the foil tray that look a bit like cat food, but actually taste OK.

So off we went. Dad even wore his best trousers, like we were going out on a special day trip. I probably wasn't any better myself by choosing to wear the most impractical boots in my limited collection. They were my bargain purchase in a charity shop a few months ago. They have huge wedges and these ridiculously long laces that threaten to whip their nearest victim into submission. But I like them. They make me feel tall and elegant (although in reality I probably look lanky and clumsy).

But things went horribly wrong so early on. I blame my Dad, as I was too busy concentrating on where his bloody faggots would be and I wasn't watching my step. This was why, when I clambered on their inclining travelator thingy (the one that you put the trolleys on), I didn't notice the lace on my stupid boots get trapped in the mechanisms on the side.

I felt myself burn up in blind panic as my foot began to be pulled backwards. My Dad, as usual, was oblivious; too busy looking at the special offers on crates of beer being advertised on the boards above us.

"Eh! Look at that. Five pound, bleedin' amazing. No need to go out these days, Maz!"

"Never mind that that! Dad, I'm stuck!"

I was pulling, but not much was happening and sweat was beginning to build. I had images of being dragged into the machine itself, my foot torn from my limb in a bloody, bony mess.

Suddenly I could see my face appearing in Take a Break or other magazines that my Mum always buys and gets all emotional over. What would be the title of my tragic story?

### *My Boots Were Made to Kill Me*

### *Tesco's Ate My Foot*

Or something equally sensational?

This drama all ended quite suddenly, when the man behind me pulled my lace out quite calmly, sighing in a patronising way that expressed quiet pity at my obvious madness.

Dad patted me on the shoulder, took my hand and led me off the travelator in a parental manner I rarely see. I swear the man behind thought he was my carer; I heard him whisper to his wife: "It must be hard for him, at his age."

After that I wanted to get out of the store as quickly as possible, my paranoia was working overtime. I had images of the security guys, hunched over their cameras, sniggering at my antics.

Dad was chuffed though. We slumped back into Norm's waiting car with just two bags, containing his beloved faggots and peas and not much else.

Ollie moaned when we got back because we had brought nothing that he had asked for.

"I might as well not live here," he moaned.

"I wish you didn't," I shot back (forgetting my promise to Jess).

"What the hell is your problem?" Ollie spat, jumping up from the sofa. "You've been nothing but off with me since I came back. Why do you hate me so much?"

Dad tried to calm the situation by pushing one of his newly purchased beers into Ollie's clenched fist.

"Calm down, son. She's always been highly strung. She's like her mother."

"No I'm not!" I shouted back. "I'm not pleased to have him back. Swanning back here after all these years of no contact. Leaving us to cope alone. Thinking he's better than everyone else!"

Ollie just looked at me, shook his head slowly and left the room.

I'm still fuming. Why can't he see why I'm angry?

Why can't he understand that I needed him? All those years I needed him and he was never there.

That's why I can't forgive him.

## Comments

**Lucy Locket:** AW, what a mixed blog. A funny story to begin with and then the horrible row.

I feel so sad for you and Ollie, can't you put the past behind you?

**MaisyM:** Sometimes I think I can and then he winds me up again. When he lived here, he was a nightmare – grumpy, angry, bossy – but at least he was here. But then he left. And Mum left. And it was just me and Dad. We never heard from him.

We struggled every day while he lived the high life.

**007:** Maybe he is sorry. Have you ever asked him? Maybe he wants to change?

**MaisyM:** Why hasn't he told me that though?

**007:** Have you ever given him the opportunity to?

## Sunday, 4th September 2011

### Mamma Mia

We went to Mum's for dinner again today as she has now decided she wants to have us a few Sundays a month. I didn't want Ollie to come, but Mum had already invited him so what choice did I have? He got up early especially.

But to be honest I think Dad was a bit put out.

"What will I have to eat?" he grumbled.

"Well, you can have those faggots you always insist we buy."

"Faggots are a Monday meal. It's Sunday today. I should be eating roast or duck or something"

"Well fry up some bacon."

"I can't do that, I might burn something..."

In the end he reluctantly (yeah, right) decided to spend the day at the Pride.

"I can make do with a bag of nuts!" he shouted as I left. "Don't fret about your dear old Dad starving, while you're tucking into your sprouts!"

On the way me and Ollie barely spoke, he was sucking hard on his cigarette and staring hard into the distance. I remember these moods from when he used to live at home. If you spoke at the wrong time he would bark at you or look at you like you were the lowest of the low.

"How's it going with with Jess?" I couldn't help but ask, as we neared Mum's place.

Ollie just shrugged. "She's a nice girl. And?"

"She's my mate," I spat back. "Anyway, isn't she a bit young for you?"

He smiled at me. "You always have to concern yourself with other people's stuff, don't you, Maz. Jess is a big girl, and we have a laugh together. Loosen up, for Christ's sake."

And then he stomped up the stairs to Mum's flat without another word.

After that, it was a bit dull at Mum's. Sweaty Keith was watching a Kung-Fu film and speaking even less than usual; he seemed mesmerised by the moves of a short man on the screen who looked as if he was constipated most of the time. And Mum was as high as a kite about the wedding. She had her laptop out and was eagerly looking at venues.

They all looked very glamorous and very expensive.

"I think it should be at the pub," Sweaty Keith said. "She keeps forgetting we're not made of money."

"Well you can think on," Mum told him.

I know, because I have often been told, that Mum's wedding to Dad had been on a shoestring, just them, two witnesses and some sandwiches at Nannas house after (who didn't approve but agreed to feed them as she didn't want to look like 'a complete bitch'). I think Mum is hoping for something more magical this time.

"Everybody wants to be special once in their lives, Maisy," she said. I guess I couldn't really argue with that.

She gave me a load of bridal magazines to take home and look through. I think she wants me to help her with ideas, but the truth is I'm useless at stuff like this. Weddings leave me a bit cold. It's always the same thing – big dress, big show-off car, big cake and big disco (usually with YMCA played at some point of the evening). Every wedding I've been to (which I admit has only been three, but that's enough to pass judgement) has had a dodgy DJ called Mike or Stevie or Rick who must have the same playlist.

Ollie might as well have not been there. He snuck past a sleeping Saffy, eyeing her up with a suspicious stare and then plonked himself down next to Sweaty Keith. Two miserable lumps together.

He also spent a lot of time texting. I wondered if it was Jess, but I didn't ask. I really didn't want to know.

If I had my way I would get married somewhere remote, pretty and quiet, and enjoy the actual point of being married without having all the fuss and bother. Of course I would have to find someone first though. I also think it would be nice to get married without having my family involved.

But then that's the difference between me and my Mum. I've wondered on several occasions whether I was adopted, and today I've become even more convinced that this could be true.

## Comments

### Lucy Locket

At least you have a wedding to look forward to.

Good luck with the job tomorrow. I have an interview for a waitressing job, not much but every bit helps

**MaisyM:** Good luck to you too!

## Tuesday 8th September 2011

### Anus Horribilis

I had been dreading the visit to the vet's, knowing that it would be horrific, traumatic and expensive.

I also had to ask Surly Sheila if I could leave work early in order to take Dave. That in itself was even more horrific, traumatic and expensive (as I lost an hour's pay). Sheila sucked in her lips and told me that I was "being quite unreasonable" and that she didn't expect this "workshy attitude from a temp."

I tried to explain to her that Dave's bottom was an urgent matter and that this was the only appointment I could get. Also, when I made the appointment, I thought 5pm was a reasonable time especially if I was working through my lunch.

Sheila said she was "disappointed in me" and she turned her head away as if she couldn't bear to look at me any longer. I felt like a repellent individual.

I was only too glad to leave.

Once home, I found Dave hiding under the dining room table. Why is it dogs have an instinct that something is going to happen that they won't like. He once tried to squeeze up the chimney when I got the worming tablets out.

I flapped his lead about in a useless attempt to fool him into thinking we were going "walkies." Dave just sunk his head lower, looking almost disappointed in me. If he could talk, he would he said "you lying cow!"

In the end I had to drag him out by the collar. Both of us were whimpering during this and at one point I almost gave up, but finally he went floppy and allowed me to apply his lead and remove him from the house.

The walk was a hard one. Dave dragged his paws in a half depressed, half defiant fashion. Every so often he would give off a pathetic yelp.

"It's not my fault your bum leaks," I hissed at him.

He looked back at me, still with his sad, pathetic 'you don't understand me' expression.

At the vets, he lay on the floor in defeat with his eyes cast down.

"Isn't he a sad old thing!" The receptionist said brightly. She annoyed me instantly; her hair was too perfect and her teeth too bright. She looked like she should be in an advert selling plug-in air fresheners.

"Wouldn't you be sad if your anal glands malfunctioned?" I shot back.

She didn't reply. Her pretty face looked all confused. I'm not sure she knew what anal glands were. Come to think of it, someone as perfect as her probably hasn't got anal glands.

Dr Keene called us in after a twenty minute wait. He was a stout man, with curly dark hair and a funny beard that looked a bit like a gerbil.

"Hello Dave," he said, patting my depressed dog, who didn't even bother to raise his head in return.

"Troublesome bottom, eh?" Dr Keene was looking at me. I felt offended for a second – my bottom was fine thank you.

I'll give him his due though, this vet didn't mess around. His gloves went on, his finger got lubricated and up it went – no messing. Dave's ears suddenly pricked up and he stared at me with a look of bewilderment. I'm not a doggy mind reader but I don't think he was impressed.

"Those glands are fine and dandy!" The vet declared joyfully, waggling his now moist glove at me. "I think the problem is more likely to be found in the bowel region."

After a quick examination of Dave's tummy and bottom, involving much prodding and poking, he deduced that Dave had Irritable bowel disorder – a nervous condition, possibly caused by stresses in his life.

"Does this dog live in a stressful environment?"

I thought about how Dad often shouts at him, the mess in the house, the general disorder that has been our life pretty much since Mum flew out of the door and onto the back of that motorbike.

"Possibly," I admitted.

So Dave is now on a prescription diet (more expense) and has to be kept away from stressful situations. I'm not sure how I will afford to keep it going. I feel like I have a permanent headache.

When I got home and relayed the news to Dad, he nearly had a fit.

"I'll give him stress! How can he be stressed? All he does is poo and sleep."

So, not unlike someone I know then…


## Comments

**Popsicle:** Irritable bowl? Poor Dave. My Auntie Claire has that and is always complaining about her grumbling bowels. She has to avoid wheaty foods

**MaisyM:** I'm not sure Dave's diet is particularly wheaty. He mainly eats out of the bin (his choice)

**Glen @LondonRiotCleanup:** Irritable Bowel? Special diet? What a pain.

It's lucky you love the dog

**MaisyM:** Yep, I do love him...

**007:** Poor old Dave, I feel sorry for him and his poorly bum. I bet he hated being poked by the vet too.

I hope he's better soon

**MaisyM:** Thank you


**Friday 9th September 2011**

## Help!!

I called Dan again today and vented my frustrations. I couldn't help myself, I felt like a pressure cooker about to explode.

"I can't do this much longer, I know it's on-going but I'm working for a monster. She is a proper mean cow."

"Oh, I'm sorry to hear that." His response sounded less chirpy, more clipped.

"No really, it's awful. She even times my loo breaks and knocks on the door if I take too long! She watches over my filing, she follows me everywhere and yesterday she told me off because I didn't 'shred straight enough.' I mean what difference does that make anyway?"

"Oh dear." He paused. "Is it really that bad?"

"Yes. And it worries me."

"Worries you?"

"Yeah, I didn't like to say before, I didn't like to make a fuss but they block the fire escapes with boxes, and I'm shredding letters that have only just been received, with 'urgent' stamped all over them. Loads of them. It all seems dodgy to me. I'm sure they're breaking a million regulations...OK, maybe not a million, but they're pretty close."

"Ok." He drew breath, I could imagine him fumbling through his papers, a small

85

frown forming. "Can you just stick it out until the end of next week? I'll try and line something else up for you. I can't promise anything mind, the market is so flat at the moment."

So that's what we agreed. I think I can manage a few more days without killing her. But the idea of spitting in her stupid, posh tea is becoming ever more appealing.

I know I'm a bad person for thinking stuff like that. But if you met her, believe me – you'd feel the same.

## Comments

**Lucy Locket:** You did the right thing babe, but I hope they can find you something else soon. There are no jobs here. Think I will be waiting tables for some time now

**Glen @LondonRiotCleanup:** Good For you. I hope the agent sorts it out

**007:** You did the right thing

There will be something else for you I'm sure.

## Monday 12ᵗʰ September 2011

### What's the best way of killing someone?

Shotgun?

Arsenic in the stupid, posh tea?

Or a stab in the back?

I could commit murder. I really, really could. It would almost be worth serving a life sentence for. It would almost be worth it, even if it meant sharing a cell with a twenty-stone woman called Bob with 'hate' tattooed across her forehead.

It actually ruined my weekend because I was so worried about work. I went to the Pride for a bit on Sunday with Jess and Poppy but it wasn't the same, I couldn't concentrate. I was just glad that Mum had cancelled on me so that she could view a venue. I don't think I could have stood a Sunday dinner at hers talking about weddings. At least me and Jess have reached a kind of mutual truce regarding Ollie; we just don't talk about him (although I can't help feeling a bit sick when I see her texting him).

I still don't understand why Ollie is bothering with Jess. I know she's pretty and acts a lot older than seventeen, but even so I would have thought she would have been too immature and unglamorous to have on the end of his arm (sorry if you read this Jess but it is the truth and I would say the same to your face).

But, like Poppy said to me, sometimes you just have to roll with these things, so that's what I'm doing, rolling. And hoping that I can be there to pick up the pieces when it all goes wrong.

I also, really really tried not to talk/think or brood about the job too much on my night out but it proved impossible.

"She's not human, that Sheila," I grumbled to the girls. "I just cannot bear to have that woman telling me one more time. 'Now Maisy, please remember you're just a temp here!' or 'Maisy, please do not smile like that, it's not appropriate,' or 'Maisy, I think three cups of tea is quite enough – don't you? That's company property you are drinking after all.'"

"She must have a sad little life," Jess decided "She must hate women, or temps, or the World."

"Maybe she is lacking love in her life?" Poppy mused.

Poppy really does think that love is the answer to everything. She would give it out on prescription if she could.

"She doesn't know the meaning of love. She only knows how to hate," I replied.

I never used to hate anyone. Not really. Except my Dad on occasions, but he has the ability to wind up a nun in a coma. But this woman brings new meaning to the word 'bitch.' She seems to thrive on being one; it must be embedded into her job description.

Poor little Becca actually shrinks when Sheila enters the room; her face drops, her shoulders slump and she appears to lose about half a stone in weight. The girl is terrified. I'm not sure how long she has worked for this witch of a boss, but if she stays there much longer she'll be a walking skeleton. I can't even to talk to her, because communication across the team is frowned upon. I will just have to hope that one day Becca will escape and find a nice little job where she can nibble biscuits and discuss what happened in Eastenders the night before. The rare, few moments when I have been able to grab a few seconds of illicit conversation with Becca, her eyes lit up like a child's on Christmas Eve. The poor thing is desperate to be released from the clutches of that job.

At least I'm just a temp. This is only a short period of hell. If I was permanent I would be climbing the walls by now.

## Comments

**Popiscle:** I still stand by what I said. Love and hate are closely linked. That woman is crying out to be loved.

**MaisyM:** Come in and give her a hug then – dare you!!

**Popiscle:** Er – no. Bit scared!!!

## Tuesday 13th September 2011

### Mrs Fiddler

Today was when I agreed to meet with Adam's mum, Mrs Fiddler. At least it was something to focus on to get through another difficult day at work.

Adam was right when he said his house was only 'down the road', as it literally was just a street away. I just wish I had had the chance to have a shower first; my armpits felt a bit mingy to say the least. I decided that I would have to keep my arms firmly clamped by my sides, just in case an ominous smell escaped. It's never good to smell like a cheese and onion pasty.

Adam's house was quite large, in a Victorian terrace. It looked a bit old and tired from the outside, but I loved the big, grand windows and warm, green door. It was nothing like our shabby house, with the broken front gate and overgrown front garden. And I really wish Dad would remove the rusty bike that leans against the wall. It's right by the door and is hardly a welcoming sight. I don't think he's even ridden it for about ten years.

This house seemed to say, 'welcome to our abode, come in!', whereas ours just says, 'bog off and don't think about it!'

Adam answered the door looking ruffled. He smiled but his face was all twitchy.

"Hello, Maisy," he said. "Come through."

Inside was not what I had imagined at all. The interior was spotless, not a speck of dirt and nothing out of place. Somehow I pictured it to be cluttered, dusty and full of curiosities. As we stood in the hall I couldn't stop staring at the gleaming black tiles on the floor. I could literally see my face in them.

Moving into the living room I began to get more nervous. The decor was entirely cream. Cream carpet, cream sofas, cream walls. Beautiful prints lined the walls and a widescreen TV (slightly larger than ours, Dad would be annoyed) sat proudly on a shiny, cream unit. Adam told me to make myself comfortable while he got his Mum.

It was then when I turned my head to the right. I couldn't quite believe what I saw. Hanging in a great, big, gilded frame, smiling for all to see, was a picture of Adam with his arms around another woman. I walked over closer to get a better look, I couldn't help myself. The girl in the photo was small and blonde with a big wide smile. Even though I wasn't that bothered about Adam, I was a bit put off having her grinning down at me like that.

"Aw, so you've seen Liz then? Isn't she a beauty?"

I turned round to find who I assumed was Mrs Fiddler, standing behind me. She was smiling faintly. I could not see the likeness between her and Adam. She was like an Empress, very tall and spindly, wearing a long, flowing dress. Her dark hair was drawn back into a tight bun, giving her quite a severe look.

I have to admit I was a little bit scared.

"Liz was Adam's last girlfriend. She was like a daughter to me." Mrs Fiddler continued in her soft tone. "Well, she still is really. We still talk every day."

"Really?" I replied. "That's nice." (No, it really wasn't!)

I looked at the photo again. This Liz was wearing a well-fitted blue dress, probably designer (it looked bloody expensive) and had a diamond necklace draped around her neck. And here was me, standing in my jeans and uniform, stinking of B.O. No contest really.

"I laid out some dinner next door; I hope you like Arrabbiata Pasta, I decided on a simple dish," she told me in her haughty manner. I noticed she emphasised the word 'simple.' "Adam's waiting there already."

We walked into the next room (and yes, that was designed in cream too) and I was surprised to find Adam sitting at the glass table already stuffing his face. Honestly, there is no nicer way of putting it. He was literally ramming the pasta into his mouth, without pausing for breath.

"Dear, dear," his mum said, sitting herself next to him (forcing me to move around the table and sit opposite him!). "He always was a hungry boy!"

"I can't help loving food," Adam replied, exposing a mouthful of congealed gunk. I wasn't feeling very hungry any more.

89

"Have some Maisy!" Mrs Fiddler continued, handing me the plate. I took a small helping and ate as daintily as I could.

"It's lovely, thank you," I said, remembering my manners.

"You must be hungry after your day," Mrs Fiddler replied. "What are you again? An Office Junior?"

She said the word, *junior*, like it was a dirty word. I could feel my hackles rising. Luckily Adam answered for me.

"She's temping for a design company, Mum!"

"Oh yes, of course. But still just an Office Junior role really." She paused. "Adam is going into management!"

"Yes, he told me," I replied sweetly. "At the newsagent's. A step up from the paper round, I guess."

There was a short silence. Mrs Fiddler was staring hard at me with her steely eyes.

"I guess," she hissed. "Anyway it's nice to have some different company today. Now Liz has gone, it gets boring just the two of us!"

Adam nodded in agreement. "But I won't move out and leave Mum," he said, as if I'd asked him (which I most certainly hadn't!). "I wouldn't like her to be on her own!"

I was starting to feel quite uncomfortable; both of them had suddenly adopted such a sickening expression of adoration in their eyes.

"We have such a close bond," his mum said, patting his hand lovingly.

"I really couldn't be without her," Adam gushed, tomato sauce dribbling down his chin.

"I believe that breast-feeding Adam until quite late has really helped to cement our loving relationship. It is the most wonderful thing you can do as a mother, Maisy. Olive?"

She stuck a bowl under my nose and I politely refused. I was feeling quite sick. My eyes kept drifting down to her boobs. Why was she telling me this? Why did she think I wanted to know?

There was a long silence and it was so uncomfortable I couldn't stand it. I began to wonder who I had come on a date with. I felt like I was eating with a bunch of freaks.

I had to revert to Action Plan A, to be used only in an emergency.

"Oh no," I said, grabbing my handbag. "My phone's going off – I can feel it vibrating. I'll be back in a second."

I went outside, and in view of Adam from the door, I had a non-existent conversation with my dead mobile. I felt like a bit of an idiot, but needs must. I couldn't continue a date with a Mummy's Boy: Who knows what he might come out with next?

Rushing back in to the dining room, I gabbled at Adam; "I'm so sorry, I have to go. My Dad needs me!" I turned to his Mum. "I'm so sorry, Mrs Fiddler. It has been a pleasure meeting you!"

"Why are you rushing off? What's happened?" Adam looked genuinely confused. I longed to whack him over the head with my bag and shout, 'Why the hell do you think I'm leaving, you ex-obsessed, Mum-obsessed, tomato-dribbler freak!'

Instead I managed to reply. "Er? He's set light to his hair. Look, you finish your lunch and I'll call you once I know what's going on."

Regrettably, Adam followed me to the door.

"Shall I call you?" he asked

"Er, nah, don't bother," I replied. "It was nice, but I... er... can't stand people who eat with their mouths open!"

And with that I raced down the path.

Although I can mark this down as an experience, I think it is fair to assume that this is probably the worst date I will EVER have.

The kebab on the way home tasted rather nice though.


## Comments

**Glen @LondonRiotCleanUp:** Ha Ha! See, I said you could do better, come on a date with me and I'll show you a good time

**MaisyM:** Lol... I think I'm giving dating a miss for a bit

**Wednesday 14th September**

**Unions have called for strike action over pensions.**

Dad said, "Here we go again, bleedin' country grinding to a halt."

He then shuffled out to watch me cook in the kitchen. "You'll have to mind when you're cooking those sausages from now on, my girl. No taking your eyes of the ball. If the firemen start striking, we'll all be left to burn. Safety must be paramount from now on."

This is coming from the man who regularly falls asleep with a cigarette clasped between his yellowed fingers.

The news also confirmed that there are now 2.5 million out of work (mainly women and young people).

That's me screwed, then.

*Comments*

**Glen @LondonRiotCleanUp:** Going to get involved in some more localised demos, this situation is crazy. The government have to sit up and listen.

**MaisyM:** I just want a decent job

**Lucy Locket:** Me too

**007:** Tough times ahead. The only way is up....

**Thursday 15th September 2011**

Just one more day! That's all! My sentence has been served.

YESSSSSSS !!!!!!!!

I'm too excited to blog. I might just do a silly dance instead...

*Comments*

**Popsicle:** We'll go out on Saturday to celebrate!!

**007:** Wish I could have seen the silly dance!

**MaisyM:** It wasn't that great, it made Dave start barking, which made Dad start shouting. I wish I hadn't bothered!


## Friday 16th September 2011

### Last Day

I woke up this morning and the birds were singing. It was like they knew and were celebrating with me. My last day at work – thank God.

Mind you, it was mixed blessings, for although I was pleased that I would never have to work with that cow-face again, I was also starting to worry that Dan wouldn't be able to find me another assignment. There really is no way I can be out of work now that I have Dave's expensive diet to maintain.

As I was walking into the office, I called Recruit4You and asked to make an appointment with my dear consultant. The wonderful receptionist answered the phone again and seemed to remember who I was. I didn't think this was a good thing,

"Ok," she said, somewhat reluctantly. "I will make you an appointment with Dan at the end of the day, 5.45pm. We look forward to seeing you then!"

What a shame she couldn't fake sincerity. She sounded like she would rather drink a pint of paint stripper than see me again this afternoon.

I arrived at MJ Design with a heavy heart. I'm also sure that the J looked even more wonky and unstable. Let's face it, if it was going to fall on anyone's head today – it was going to be me.

Sheila was waiting for me by the door, hands on hips (her favoured position).

"So I understand you're leaving us today," she barked. "Not to worry, I'm sure that useless agency will send me another witless temp."

"I'll be sorry to go," I lied

"No you won't. You hate it, I can see. It's written all over your face."

God, I can't tell you how much I hate this woman. She's wasted in this place; she should be working for a dictatorship somewhere, brandishing a whip. Whips were designed to be held by someone as nasty and vindictive as her.

93

As usual, my first task was to make her a cup of Earl Grey tea. Standing in the kitchen, my eyes were drawn to the tub of bright yellow washing-up liquid. On the label it promised to "add brightness to your day."

Well, I figured a small squirt in her foul smelling cup might actually help to cheer her up a bit. I didn't wait to see her reaction as she took a sip. Her taste buds are so hardened, she probably didn't even notice.

Today, my job was mainly based around filing the last boxes of crap that had been stuffed under desks and hidden away in cupboards. From what I could gather, I think they were personnel files and records. I'm not sure why they hadn't been sorted before now. Most of the filing cabinets were fit to bursting, so squeezing the files inside meant bending and buckling the majority of them, but I had gone past caring what damage was being caused. Sod them. They could all buckle and break for all I cared.

I just switched off and drifted into my happy place, something I've got used to doing over the years.

At four in the afternoon, I decided I needed a loo break. I walked quickly past Sheila (who was filing her long, red talons) and told her politely where I was going.

"Don't be long!" She shouted across the office. "Remember, time is money!"

Locking the door in the poky cubicle, I plonked down on the hard, cold seat and did my business. I then dug my mobile phone out of my trouser pocket and tapped out a message to Jess. I had no intention of rushing, not today. My bladder was on strike.

*This is hell. Save me, pls*

She replied in seconds.

*Know how u feel, really wanna leave this dull shop job and do beauty course but no funds x*

Jess still wanted to do her beauty course, but the cost was beyond her. Her Mum wasn't prepared to stump up the money, so it looked as though she was stuck where she was for a while longer.

It's so crap being seventeen (or eighteen in Jess's case, as she never fails to remind us). We used to moan about school, but that was much better than being in the kind of limbo land that we're in now.

I leaned back against the wall and waited, it didn't take long for the banging on the door to start.

"Maisy! You have been four minutes already. I know this is your last day, but this is ridiculous."

"I'm doing a poo!" I yelled back. "A big, fat poo!"

"Maisy!" She sounded shocked. Does she not poo then? Does she have it all sucked out of her, twice a week in a special poo clinic somewhere?

"I'm so sorry, but it's stuck!" I shouted. "I'll be out as soon as I can squeeze it out!"

There was no reply, but I knew she was sucking in her cheeks, her face reddening at my coarse tone. How dare I say 'poo' to her? How dare I even contemplate taking ten minutes in the toilet!

For that's how long I took, sitting with my eyes shut, calmly breathing in the scent of toilet freshener and dreaming of being somewhere, anywhere but here.

When I left the cubicle, I sailed past Sheila and her disgusted face.

"You might want to leave it five minutes before going in…" I told her sweetly.

I left an hour later with barely a goodbye from my new enemy; she just glanced up at me and waved lazily. Becca, sitting nervously beside her, smiled meekly, almost in apology. I felt sorry for her having to stay there. Having to do this job day in day out, no wonder she looks so bloody miserable.

"Good luck," Sheila said with a fake smile, her eyes cold and hard.

I wonder why she hated me so much. I have the feeling that she feels this way about most temps.

I staggered into Recruit4You feeling tired and de-motivated. Sue was at the desk waiting for me with a sugary smile.

"Dan is waiting for you!" she said, pointing over to his desk and then she went back to the magazine she was reading.

Dan was indeed sitting there, still under a pile of paperwork. He beckoned me over and I plonked myself down opposite him.

"All finished then?" he said.

"Yep, I pity the poor fool that goes in there next."

Dan sighed. "Yeah…thing is you highlighted some issues about health and safety and stuff. I think I will need to pay them a visit before I send anyone else there."

I nodded, pleased.

"Anyway," Dan continued. "As I said on the phone, there's not much about at the moment. But I know you need the money, so…"

"So?"

"Would you be happy being a chamber-maid? It's a hotel in town. Early morning shifts, so your afternoons will be your own. But it can be dirty work."

"That's fine," I replied. "I'm used to dirty work."

Dan smiled at me and began to print out the details of the assignment to start on Tuesday. I was pleased to hear that once again it was on-going. While I was waiting, I looked around the office. Only Stella was there, and she was busy typing. She was sat very erect with perfect posture, her pretty little face the picture of concentration.

Dan caught me looking and smiled shyly at me.

"We're thinking about moving in together soon," he whispered. "Big changes for me!"

Stella turned as if she heard us talking and flashed a bright, beaming smile at Dan. He turned back to the computer screen looking almost nervous.

"Big changes…" he whispered again, but this time I think he was talking to himself, not to me.


## Comments

**Glen @ LondonRiotCleanUp:** Yeah! You're out! I hope the agency close them down

**Popiscle:** So glad you're out of there. Chambermaiding will be ok. At least you'll have afternoons off.

**Lucy Locket:** A lot of my mates do chambermaiding. Good luck!

**007:** You'll be fine. This one will be better!

**MaisyM:** Thank you guys! Xxx

## Friday 23rd September 2011

### Strike

It was a bad start this morning. I woke to find Ollie in the kitchen surrounded by more bin bags.

"She just left my stuff outside the door again. Anyone could have taken it. Why would she do that do me?" He wailed. "I thought she would come here with my stuff in cases. I thought we could talk."

I think he was even more pissed off that his laptop was still nowhere in sight.

"I bet the cow has sold it for another Botox treatment," he ranted. "The stupid cow has had so much work done; she's about as expressive as a Barbie doll."

Dad was slumped on his armchair, a look of pure dejection on his face. I knew something bad had happened because he had the same depressed look on his face that he had had when Mum left. He never looks like that normally, unless he has been hitting the gin.

"What's wrong, Dad?" I asked eventually. "You've got a look about you that would turn milk. Didn't you have a good night last night?"

"Stop worrying about him! His troubles are nothing compared to mine!" Ollie blasted. "Doesn't anyone care how I'm feeling?"

"I'm on strike as of today," Dad muttered, ignoring Ollie's ranting. "I will never, ever enter that pub again! Last night was my last night."

"Why? What happened?"

"Jimmy's been sacked," he replied. "They said he was stealing the food. It's all lies. I think he only took peanuts. I mean, who gives a toss about peanuts?"

"Oh, poor Jimmy."

"Yes, poor Jimmy. Well, I'm in protest. I've not felt this way since the poll tax riots." He shouted; "They won't be getting my custom now!"

"Oh Dad, Jimmy wouldn't expect that of you!"

"But it's all going to change Maz, don't you see? New bloody management, new bloody rules. Quiz nights will be gone, to be replaced by karaoke. They'll spruce up the place, make it look all flash and shiny. It won't be a local any more, it'll be another bloody knocking shop!"

"You don't know that. The new manager could be another bloke like Jimmy!" I protested, trying to make him feel better.

"Oh no!" he said, shaking his head. "They've already appointed his replacement. A bloody woman, would you believe?"

"And what's wrong with a woman running things?" I asked, feeling slightly put out.

"Nothing, except she's bound to mess it up. There are some things women weren't gifted to manage, and pubs are one of them!"

I was beginning to see why Mum left him for the bloke with the long nose. I bet he wasn't a sexist pig. I bet he didn't sit in a stained armchair spouting rubbish.

"Not only that, Norm saw her looking around yesterday."

"And? What was she like?"

"All he said was that she was small and suspicious looking. Well, balls to that!" Dad sat back further in his chair. "I'm not setting foot in there again; it's a matter of principle."

"Are you going to form a picket line?" asked Ollie dryly, who was still rummaging through his black bags.

"My picket line is this house and I'm not crossing it!" Dad replied. "Anyway, that's not all that's troubling me. According to Norm, there is a ruddy great satellite heading our way. It's due to hit Earth on Monday."

"You what?" Ollie looked up, worried.

"They reckon this huge satellite that the Americans stuck up in space years ago and forgot about is now heading our way." Dad pointed absently up at the ceiling. "Apparently there is a 1-3000 chance that the bloody thing will hit somebody. Can you imagine that? You could be fast asleep, or in the middle of a big poo and then BOOM! That's it – that's your head gone!"

"I'm sure it would be more than your head gone…" Ollie muttered, still looking concerned.

"But what a way to go. And would you see it coming? Would you have time to duck?" Dad was obviously pondering. "It's worrying me. I like to know what I'm facing. I have plans, you know."

"Do you?" I couldn't help asking.

Dad ignored this. "If the blighter lands on my shed, I'm suing the Yanks," he declared.

At least I had a night out at the Pride tonight with Jess and Poppy. To be honest, I couldn't afford much else.

We went to Poppy's to get ready. Jess smuggled in a bottle of cheap wine and helped Poppy dig something reasonable out of the back of her cupboard. I still think I look bland and gangly in comparison to those too.

Jess was a bit quiet tonight, because she had found out that Steve had been given community service for his part in the riots. Apparently he cried like a baby in the dock.

"Do you care?" I asked her. "I thought you weren't interested in him anymore."

Jess just shrugged. "I don't like to think of him being upset, that's all."

"But you and Ollie?"

"Me and Ollie are just having a laugh. He's really easy to talk to... but...."

"But, what?"

I was intrigued. This was the first time Jess had ever revealed anything about Ollie to me.

Jess shook her head. "It's nothing really, I just wonder if he's holding something back. Now enough about me, let's talk about other stuff!"

Poppy was happy to do this as she was a high as a kite. In fact, she was so bloody annoying and giggly, I thought she had been overdosing on Jelly Tots again.

"It's my book," she explained, lying back on my bed. "It's nearly finished I think and I have a feeling it's going to be huge!"

"Good for you, hun, c'mon let's get to the Pride," Jess replied, almost dismissively.

As it was, our evening turned out to be quite disappointing as Jess said she was feeling tired and sick, and Poppy suddenly realised that she had 'worked out a new ending.' So I found myself up walking home before ten feeling quite deflated.

On the way back, I saw Ollie standing outside our house on his mobile phone, obviously ranting at someone as he was gesticulating quite aggressively.

As I approached him I heard him say: "And this goes no bloody further, right!" He snapped shut the phone and stormed back into the house.

I waited a while before going back in, sensing something wasn't right. He was obviously wound up with someone and I wasn't even sure I wanted to know why.

I couldn't help looking up at the sky for a moment, wondering if this satellite was above my head right at that moment.

Knowing my luck it will be my head it lands on. I wonder if anyone will notice?

## Comments

**Glen @LondonRiotCleanup:** Hmm, intriguing. I wonder who your brother has upset?

BTW that satellite won't land on your Dad's shed – chances are it will end up at the bottom of the Pacific...

**MaisyM:** Yeah, but my luck ain't great....

**007:** I'm more worried about your Dad giving up the Pride; how will he cope?

**MaisyM:** God knows. How will I cope?

**SkySpotter22:** Hey Maisy – Follow us tonight on Twitter, we can tell you the exact location of the UARS satellite as it falls.

**MaisyM:** Cool – might just do that

## Sunday 25th September 2011

### Wedding Planner

This morning when I got up it was just me and Dad. Ollie was obviously still sleeping in. I was so relieved that I wasn't working as I had a stonking headache and had to raid the medicine cabinet for drugs.

"How was it?" Dad muttered.

He was sat watching some political programme and actually stroking the dog. He looked old in his faded pyjamas.

"It was OK," I said. I wasn't really sure how to answer. I didn't want to tell him that the pub was heaving. He would hate to know that all the regulars were there and that they had been holding a darts match that he would have loved. Surely that would have been taunting a man on strike?

"What is she like?" he asked, not looking away from presenter on the TV, who was waving his arms about in a rather haphazard fashion; he looked like he might knock someone out at any minute.

"She seemed nice, friendly," I told him.

Debs Flannigan, the new landlady had actually come over to introduce herself to us. She was lovely, very small with long, dark hair and a slightly brassy manner. She must have been in her late fifties, but she had an elegance and grace that made her look younger.

"She's not very suspicious looking," I added. "But she is small, tiny in fact."

"Never trust a small woman," Dad muttered. "Huge tempers."

"Norm is having his 60th birthday bash there two weeks Saturday. He wants you to be there."

"I'm on strike."

"He's your oldest friend."

"I'm on strike, I have my principles."

"It's a free bar."

Dad didn't reply but I'm sure I could hear the whirl of his brain. That was a huge thing, a free bar. That was something he could never refuse.

I left him alone to digest the information and got ready to go to Mum's.

Unfortunately, Ollie crawled out of bed in time to come with me.

"I won't miss a roast," he yawned, scratching his balls.

This time when we arrived at Mum's, Saffy was being held quite tightly by Sweaty Keith so there was no risk of an attack taking place, which was a damn shame really. That was the highlight of last week.

Mum was very excited. She had a load of wedding brochures out on her dining room table and beckoned us round to have a look.

"We want to get married sooner rather than later," she explained. "Ideally in December because that is my very favourite month."

That's the first I've heard of it. Last December all Mum did was complain because it snowed and she kept slipping in her stupidly high heels. I'm certain she even said, 'I really hate winter.'

I'm sure the truth is that she is rushing the wedding because she is terrified that Sweaty Keith will change his mind, and judging by the look on his pale face this might not be such a mad assumption.

"I want to pick winter flowers. Reds and whites – maybe some berries!" she said, prodding at a picture of a huge bouquet. It looked a bit ugly and prickly but I didn't like to say.

"And I would love for you to come dress shopping with me, Maisy. You will, won't you?"

"Of course. Have you got any ideas?"

"Well, I don't like to say too much in front of Keith but..." She leant forward and whispered, "*I'm thinking dark red and very low cut.*"

I nodded. "Sounds lovely."

Ollie was standing there idly leafing through the magazines. "So, are you having a rolls or a horse drawn carriage, Mum?" he asked dryly.

"Neither," shouted Sweaty Keith from the other side of the living room, where he was watching the Belgian Grand Prix. (I've never got that, what's the attraction in a load of cars going up and down a great big road? You might as well just stand over the bridge on the M25, and you're probably likely to see far more crashes.)

"He's right," Mum said. "I'm going in a motorcycle sidecar. How romantic is that?"

"Lovely," said both me and Ollie in unison, and we looked at each other surprised when we did.

Mum nipped into the kitchen to check on her Roast Lamb and then shouted back into us: "I haven't told you the best bit yet!"

"What's that?" I asked, trying to sound enthusiastic.

"I want you to be my bridesmaid, Maisy!"

"Oh....Thanks," I replied, not really sure what to say. I've only been bridesmaid once before and that was for my cousin Louise (I was ten). I had to wear a frilly pink thing and I looked more like a fancy bog-roll holder rather than a bridesmaid.

"Mum, please don't make me wear anything pink or fussy…"

"Of course I won't!" she shouted back. "Anyway, I was thinking more peach!"

Ollie was smirking beside me. "Peach will be so becoming!" he hissed at me. "Why don't I suggest lemon or lime green?"

"Shut it," I hissed back.

"That's not all of it," Mum said, walking back into the room, brandishing a wooden, pastry baster in an excitable way. "Ollie – we would like you to be the pageboy."

"What the hell?" Ollie looked up from the magazine he been flicking through. "You want me to be WHAT?"

"I would like you to be my pageboy. I know that they are usually little. But it's my wedding and I want a big one."

"Hang on a minute Mum, let me get this straight. You want me to dress up in a sailor suit? I'm twenty-bloody-six!"

"Not a sailor suit, no, but maybe a nice dickie bow and tails," she replied. "And watch your language!"

It was my turn to start laughing. "Peach isn't looking so bad now is it?" I whispered back.

"I'm beginning to wonder why the hell I bothered to come home," he grumbled.

"You're not the only one," I muttered.

He glared back at me and then went back to his magazine. He barely spoke for the rest of the day. I think the whole thing had really got to him.

I think I might try and push Mum on that Sailor Suit idea after all…

And just for the record that bloody satellite didn't hit anything, it landed in the ocean (they think). Just like many things, it was a great big drama over nothing.


**Comments**

**Glen @ LondonRiotCleanup:** Sailor suit!! ROFL!!

**007:** Poor Ollie, not sure I'd be up for that.....

**MaisyM:** Think it's funny personally!!

**007:** You're too cruel ;o)

**Lucy Locket:** I do feel sorry for him. He won't want to look like a tit on his Mum's big day. Are you going to tell Jess about the phone call you overheard yesterday?

**MaisyM:** Nah, gonna leave it. She might read it on here anyway, but I doubt it because she said she'd never read this blog again. I think I have to leave them to get on with it.

**Glen @LondonRiotCleanup:** I'm still laughing about your bro!

But at least the satellite didn't break your dad's shed – or your head! And I think you're doing the right thing about Jess. Sometimes you just have to let things be.


**Monday 26th September 2011**

**Walking the Demented Dog**

Today I decided to be pro-active and energetic on one of my last days before I start the new job. I decided to take Dave for a long walk.

Dave doesn't get taken out much because, unlike most dogs, Dave doesn't like walking. Come to think of it, he's more like my Dad than I'd appreciated. Dave also hates getting wet and if he detects even a hint of rain, he will dive into the nearest bush and hide there until the shower passes.

When you take him out, he plods alongside you reluctantly in a 'well, if I have to' manner. It's quite off-putting really, makes me wonder why I bother. Today was no exception. Dave was stomping next to me, all heavy-footed. When we got to the play park, he took one look around and then laid down in disgust. It took a few gentle prods with my boot to get him moving again.

It's not fair. I see other dog owners, with their animals and they are having loads of fun. Dave wouldn't know what fun was if it came and bit him on the nose.

I'm actually starting to wonder if my dog might be depressed. Can an irritable bowel make you depressed? I'm sure it can't be too nice to have problems 'downstairs' all the time, or have my Dad calling you 'a stinky arse mutt' every five minutes. Dad won't be sympathetic to Dave's problems. He just laughs and says the dog should take up 'yoga' to relieve his stress.

"The day he's been signing on the dole queue for six years, with no hope of a job, struggling with back pain and having his wife up and leave him for a man with a face like a wind suck, is the day I will accept that he MIGHT have depression," Dad stated the other evening.

I'm beginning to think Dad might have issues too.

I decided to try and cheer Dave up by throwing a stick. I've been told that it's the wrong thing to do (in case it splinters in their throats) so please don't tell me off, dog lovers out there!! It really is the only thing that Dave will run and fetch. Maybe he has a 'thing' for wood.

And it did do the trick. His little ears pricked up once I'd thrown the stick back and forth a few times. He was even panting a little bit, which is a rare thing for Dave. I decided to go for another big throw, and managed to lob the stick into a small thicket of bushes.

Clumsy Dave ran in head first, scurried around for a bit and then returned to me – not with the stick I had thrown, but with a ruddy great log about twice the width that he was.

It was so big that Dave was struggling to carry it, but he was so pleased with himself. He was looking at me, waiting for praise, like he had just hunted down some prey.

"Drop it Dave!" I commanded, in my best bossy voice.

Dave just looked at me as if I was a lunatic and then decided, for the first time in his stupid life, to leg it in the opposite direction.

Now, I have to admit that a dog with a massive log in his mouth cannot move at great speed. However, neither can a girl who had just consumed a Mars Bar and a can of Coke and had a horrible stitch in her side because of it.

Dave, typically, was hurtling towards a group of mothers sitting in a neat little ring, eating a picnic. Their little darlings were toddling around them and unfortunately were in the direct line of Dave's careering path.

"Dave, No!" I screamed, but it was too late. My stupid dog and his massive log had managed to knock one small girl clean off her feet (lucky she had a nappy on and had a soft landing).

Dave also decided to stamp over several sandwiches and delicately laid out baby biscuits, before crashing out, a panting lump a few yards away.

I stood mortified while one of the Mums picked up the fallen child (who by the way was not crying, she had by now been distracted by a blade of grass). This Mum swept the baby up in her thin, tanned arms and then marched towards me.

"Your dog is a danger to the public," she spat. "It could have killed my Alice."

"I don't think..."

"That thing in his mouth; if that had made contact with the soft part of her head, well, that would have been it, no more Alice," she informed me.

"Even so, it didn't and it was an accident and I really am sorry," I garbled back.

The woman looked at me with disgust. She didn't look like any Mummy I knew, but then again most of the Mum's I know are on benefits and struggling to get by. This Mummy had designer jeans that looked as if they had been air-brushed on, her t-shirt was beautifully cut and her hair had been cut well and blow-dried into style.

"Perhaps if you got a job, instead of loitering around parks," she sneered. "At eighteen I was doing my degree. I had direction. All I see now is the likes of you, hanging around with nothing better to do than bother us!"

She flapped her hand loosely at her friends, who all looked as perfect and well designed as her.

"I have got a job..."

I started to say, but she was already walking away, comforting her already contented child.

I wanted to say, *"I've got a job and if I had my way I would be doing a degree, but I don't fancy being in debt for the rest of my life trying to pay it back and even then I'm not guaranteed a job."*

I wanted to say, *"Who the hell are you to judge me or anyone else when you've had everything handed to you on a plate. Perhaps me, and others like me, come to parks because there's nothing else to do."*

I could have said, *"Piss off you ugly, dried up old cow. And by the way your baby looks like a Pokemon."*

But I didn't. Instead I prodded Dave awake again (after hiding his log) and walked slowly home, hating my life and wondering if it was ever going to get better.


## Comments

**Glen @LondonRiotCleanup:** Your life is fine. Times are tough for many of us at the moment. Don't take any notice of these snobs.

**MaisyM:** Sometimes I just wish things were different

**Glen@LondonRiotCleanup:** Don't. You are what you are. It will only make you stronger.

**Popsicle:** And we all love you for it.


## Wednesday 28th September 2011

### Maid in Croydon

Ollie is getting worse. When the hell is he going to get a job? Or give us some money towards food? Or do something useful? All he seems to do is hang around the house like a bad smell. Or go to the pub with Dad. Or go and see Jess. It's so depressing.

He looked at me with scorn when I was leaving to start my first shift at the Grange. I was being eased in gently by being asked to start at 8am (which sounded horrific enough). The usual start is at 6am, so I'm going to have to get used to early mornings. Either that or I won't bother going to bed in the first place. After all, Dad does it all the time.

"Have fun making beds!" Ollie shouted as I left.

I ignored him, leaving with my head held high.

*What exactly happened to your fantastic job, Ollie? You never did quite explain, did you....*

I had to walk to the Grange. I didn't know the hotel well, but had passed it a few times. It was a fairly large, non-descript and pretty unimpressive red-brick, three-storey building with a basic side extension. The front was a large, tarmac car park with a few potted plants dotted about.

I walked into reception and the lady there was friendly enough. She had a wide smile which was a blessing for me. She introduced herself as the manager, Monica, and showed me into a big laundry room downstairs where I had to load up a trolley with cleaning stuff. I didn't have the privilege of wearing a uniform, as I was just a temp.

"You won't be working alone for the first few weeks," Monica told me, her bright eyes shining. "I'll pair you up with Alice, so that you will have someone to show you the ropes. Alice has been here for years so will be able to get you up and running in no time. We'll go and find her now. I believe she has already started work on the first floor."

The two of us lugged this hefty old trolley onto the lift and made our way to Alice. I was feeling strangely nervous, like I was going on a blind date or something.

Alice was found in room 115. She was a tiny woman, extremely bony, with long, straw-like hair pulled into a tight ponytail. She looked older than me, I was guessing in her late twenties.

"I'll leave you two to get along," Monica said in her jolly way, pushing aside her long, grey hair. "I expect you'll finish at about eleven, so I will see you then!"

Alice turned to me and gave me a sly smile. She had a very ruddy face.

"Hello," she said. "What do you wanna do? Beds or bogs?"

Not surprisingly I plumped for beds. Alice gave me a quick run-through of what was expected. It was tougher than I thought. Stripping, re-making, pulling everything tight. Even after the first bed, my back was beginning to ache. This certainly wasn't the office temp job I had dreamed of.

"It gets easier," Alice told me kindly, noticing my expression.

We didn't talk much as we did the rest of the rooms, although Alice did switch on cable TV most of time, so at least I had some music to listen to as I worked. Alice was very quiet and if I asked her questions, she would just give one word answers or grunts. I guess she just doesn't like talking much.

At the end of the shift, Monica asked me what I thought.

"It was OK," I replied, although honestly I felt hot, dirty and exhausted. I also wished that Alice had been a bit chattier.

I just wanted to climb back into bed again and sleep for the rest of the afternoon.


### Comments

**007:** Glad your first day went well. I'm sure you'll get the hang of it in no time. At least it keeps you out of the mad house

**MaisyM:** Well...that's' true!

**Popsicle:** Hope it gets easier!

BTW I'm sending you the 1st draft of Miss Stake. Maybe you can take a peek?

**MaisyM:** OK. No probs

**Popiscle:** Thanks babe

I was talking to Jess today. Apparently Steve is sniffing around again.

**MaisyM:** Really? Is she interested?

**Popsicle:** Not sure...you know Jess. Keeps options open ;o)


**Friday 30th September 2011**

**Mate Date**

Today I decided to pop over and see Jess after work. She had a day off, so was still lounging in her bright pink PJ's when I arrived.

"It's okay for her," her Mum, Stella, barked in her direction. "Some of us have to show some motivation."

Stella Bridges always scares me a little bit, she has incredibly short hair that is a different colour every time I see her and she has these weird bulbous eyes that follow you around everywhere you go. Jess always calls her 'the paranoid freak,' probably not the nicest thing to call you Mum – but Jess and Stella have a kind of 'love/hate relationship.' It borders on hate a lot of the time.

Stella was currently trying to re-paint her hall and not making a very good job of it. She had more paint on her body than on the walls. I felt a bit sorry for her. It was a bit bad of Jess not to be helping.

Jess was too pre-occupied watching Deal or No Deal.

"Look at his jumper!" she laughed when I walked in. "Dead sad. That has to rank as the worst jumper ever."

I plonked myself down next to her. There is always something comforting about sitting next to Jess, she always has the same sweet smell about her.

I guess I've always looked up to Jess. We've been friends since primary school even though she was a year older than me. It helped having her at secondary school because she was older and knew all the 'hard kids.' I really missed her in my last year at school when she had left, and it was just me and gentle Poppy. Suddenly I was more exposed to Melissa Henderson and her mates.

I'm not sure why Jess stayed close to me and Poppy, I think she just genuinely enjoys our company, even though she treats us like her kid sisters sometimes.

"You had a good day off?" I asked her.

"S-alright," she grunted. "I'm just glad to be away from that shop for a bit, its making me brain dead. I've told Mum I want to start a College course."

"Really? What did she say?"

"That I never settle into anything. That I'm fickle. That I don't know what I want. She's an idiot....I know I want to do beauty therapy."

"I'm sure she'll listen eventually."

Jess shrugged, she didn't look too concerned. She usually gets her own way.

"Poppy said that Steve's hanging around again," I said casually.

Jess didn't look away from the TV.

"Yeah, he's been creeping around again. Says he misses me and all that. Keeps saying that he's changed."

"Do you believe him?"

She shrugged again. I noticed she was nibbling her lip quite hard.

""Does he know about Ollie?"

"Not sure."

"So what will you do?"

It was then Jess turned away from the screen and faced me, smiling.

"What will I do, Maisy? I will do absolutely nothing! I'm just having fun. I'm not hurting anyone. I'm not obligated to anyone. I'm just going to see how things go."

"Oh, as long as you're sure?"

"Jesus girl, you really need to chill out."

I sat back on the sofa and began to wonder whether Jess was right: Am I taking things too seriously?

"You should get a nice jumper like his, hun! You're ancient like him..."

And then she hit me with a cushion, so I think I was forgiven.

## Comments

**Lucy Locket:** I would probably be thinking the same, so don't feel too bad. It's called being a worrier

**MaisyM:** Thank you! I'm glad I'm not alone

**007:** But maybe you need to ease up and not get too concerned. Sometimes you have to let people make their own mistakes.

Please don't start wearing Noel Edmunds jumpers though!

**MaisyM:** Ha ha, I'm not that sad yet!

**007:** I bet you could pull off the look...

**MaisyM:** Doubtful...;o)

**Funnygirl3:** Great blog BTW, just started following.


## Sunday 2nd October 2011

### Mum's Music

Today was dinner at Mum's again. I think my body is adjusting to the new routine, because my stomach was growling with anticipation as soon as I woke up.

I largely ignored Ollie over breakfast; he was too busy texting anyway. I assumed it was Jess because of the soppy look on his face.

"You're wasting your time with her," I snapped. "She goes through men quicker than Imodium."

"Who said I was texting your mate?" he asked, raising an eyebrow at me.

"You're just messing around with her until something better comes along, aren't you?"

"And so what if I am? What's the harm in the two of us having a little fun?" Ollie got up and threw his bowl casually into the sink. "You just need to loosen up a bit, sis and get your large nose out of my business."

Idiot. And yet *another* dig at my nose (is it really that big?).

I didn't even wait for him today and walked over to Mum's on my own. Stuck my battered old I-Pod in my ears (second hand from Poppy when she upgraded) and tried to chill out listening to some tunes. I didn't notice him coming up behind me and when he tapped me on the back I ignored him. He fell into step with me and we walked the entire way in silence.

I do wonder sometimes if it will always be like this. If we will end up two old and bitter people, sitting on our battered mobility scooters, still ignoring each other, apart from the odd spiteful comment. Will we still hate each other for reasons that we don't even know?

It's a good job that Mum's flat is always so, well, filled with Mum's excitement and banter. Mum tends to ignore the negative atmosphere and the glum faces and pretends that everyone loves each other (apart from her and Dad, they are allowed to be sworn enemies of course).

Mum had the music blaring when we walked in. Sweaty Keith was sat on the floor surrounded by CDs. Saffy was hiding under the table, obviously in protest at the crap music that was being blasted out.

"Maisy! Ollie!" She screamed above the deafening throb, before deciding it might be wise to turn the volume down a bit. "We're picking music for the wedding. You two can help. I need some young influence."

She certainly did need help if she was planning to play Bat out of Hell at the reception.

"Mum. Have you listened to these lyrics at all? This is hardly appropriate to play on your wedding day?"

"Eh?" Mum looked confused.

"It goes 'like a bat out of hell I'll be gone before the morning comes. When the night is over and the sun comes out, I'll be gone, gone, gone!" I sang along (badly).

"But this is my very favourite song," said Sweaty Keith bleakly from his perch on the floor. I looked down at his sad little face and felt almost sorry for him.

"It might be your favourite song, but the message is a bit – well – mixed? Surely you have other songs?"

"What about 'Creep'?" asked Ollie, straight faced. "That always gets the old girls up dancing. Or 'The Drugs don't Work' – probably quite apt in this case?"

"Ollie, you're not helping," I shot back.

"I love Mad World, but the Tears for Fears version," Sweaty Keith said hopefully.

"Again, it's not really a wedding song; think of something loving, romantic?" I suggested.

"Total Eclipse of the Heart!" Mum screamed. "Everybody loves a bit of Bonnie Tyler at a wedding, don't they?"

"Oh look," said Ollie calmly, looking through the CD's. "Suicide is Painless. Play this one for me. It might help when I'm walking around on the day dressed like a complete TWAT!"

"Ollie," Mum said softly as if she was telling off a small boy. Ollie slumped himself in a chair, obviously sick of the conversation.

"I need a first dance song," Mum continued, still rifling through her collection. "That is the most important song of the night."

"Well, what's your song? You must have a song?" I said, trying to be helpful.

"It's Achy Breaky Heart," chirped up Sweaty Keith again, with an essence of pride. "I sang that to your mother on karaoke the night we met. It's kind of stuck."

We finally agreed that more thought would need to be put into this decision. I said that I would borrow some naff romantic CDs off Poppy for them both to listen to. With any luck they should be able to find a suitable song amongst that lot.

Later in the kitchen, Mum grabbed my arm.

"I just want everything to be perfect, Maisy," she hissed. "And that means you and Ollie getting along. I hate to see the two of you so frosty with each other."

"I'm surprised you've noticed," I muttered back.

"Of course I've noticed, I'd be bloody blind, stupid or your bloody Dad not to notice. Just try and get along with him. For my sake."

I hate it when she asks things like that of me. I want to shout back 'why the hell should I do anything for you, when it was you that left us.' It's her fault our family is so messed up. She should be thankful I can forgive her for that, not be asking favours from me.

But I know I will try. Because that's what I always do.

I went home feeling quite angry and then ended up lying on my bed crying my eyes out. I hate the way my family make me feel.

## Comments

**Lucy Locket:** Aw don't cry!

I loved the song suggestions. Bat out of Hell – lol!

**007:** You should get them to have their first dance to the Lazy Song

**Glen@LondonRiotCleanup:** Or Duck Sauce

**007:** Or Do it Like a Dude....

**MaisyM:** You guys are no help xo)!!

**Popiscle:** Don't worry babe – I have loads of CD's your Mum can borrow

## Monday 3rd October 2011

### Marching Nanna

I guess I should have wondered why I hadn't heard from Nanna for a bit. I thought she might have called me after the Kev Kirby night – if only to mock it some more. But to be honest – although we try to have regular calls (and when I can be naffed, visits) – Nanna does tend to wander off for days on end, usually on some mission or another.

Today, however, we got a bit of a shock when watching the afternoon news. I was flopped out after another back-breaking shift, cursing Dan for giving me the most exhausting work on earth! Dad was in a bad mood anyway, complaining about his bad back (but I think the truth is he is missing the Pride; by all accounts the new landlady is doing a great job there).

The coverage was of the four-day Conservative Party conference in Manchester. Dad had been following it on and off on Sky, mainly so that he could shout abuse on the odd occasion.

The footage was showing coverage of the marches that took place yesterday. The newsreader was dryly announcing that "more than 35,000 had taken part in the march that had centred in the main parts of Manchester, protesting against government cuts."

It looked like fun, this 'March for the Alternative' – although I'm not quite sure what the alternative is. I think I'm beginning to believe Dad is right when he says they should sling the whole lot out and start again. This time with *real* people who actually know what it's like to be out of work or struggling on benefits.

The newsreader (who looked as though he had a bad cold judging by his red nose) went on to say that "people were angry."

Really? Funny that...

"I wish I could be there, Maisy," my Dad was moaning. "And I would be too, if it wasn't for my back. Power to the people and all that. I was there for the Poll Tax marches. This is Maggie all over again...I tell you now, I...what the flippin hell..."

Dad actually leapt out of his chair (his back looking particularly strong) and started pointing at the TV in excitement.

"Isn't that Bab's demented Mum?" Dad yelled. "Your bleedin Nanna?"

The news was focused on two hundred or so people sitting in a small area, obviously staging their own protest. Amongst them, indeed was my 'bleedin Nanna.' She was sitting quite upright in the centre, her white hair sparkling in the light. She looked quite regal.

The newsreader obviously thought so too, because he homed in on her, with his rather oversized microphone.

"So what brings you here today, Madam?"

"My bloody principles, that's what," she replied in her stern fashion. "This country is being done over and I want to make my feelings heard."

The newsreader, obviously flustered at the bad language tried to move away, but not before my Nanna was caught saying: "But sitting on my arse on this cold floor is sodding my piles up a treat..."

I think my Dad has new found respect for her.


**Comments**

**Glen @LondonRiotCleanup:** I LOVE YOUR NANNA

I'm recruiting her as patron of our charity. She rocks

**Funnygirl3:** She is so cool. My nan is evil and blows smoke in my face. Can we swap?

**007:** You could loan her out. She makes *me* proud

**MaisyM:** She worries me...


## Tuesday 4th October 2011

### Breaking Back

Dan called me today, after my shift, to ask how it was going. I was walking home slightly awkwardly as my back was aching so much. I never thought I was a lazy cow, but this is definitely hard work. Alice, who still isn't talking much, has assured me that my spine will harden up. Her back was obviously as strong as steel, but then again she had been doing the job for six years.

I've popped into the Co-op and bought some reduced Radox. I'm going to soak in that for an hour tonight – and sod Ollie if he starts banging on the door because he wants to do his hair, he can just get lost.

"How's my favourite temp doing?" Dan asked. He sounded like his smarmy old self this time.

"Not bad. Aching a bit, but it could be worse. I think I can stick this one out."

There was a short intake of breath – I knew then that something bad was coming. He wasn't ringing me to say that I had been awarded an extra penny an hour on my minimum wage.

"Actually Maz, I think this will only be a few weeks work – tops! I'm on the case, trying to find you something else."

"But you said it would be on-going?"

"I thought it would. Trouble is the hotel chain is making cutbacks, and temps are always the first to go."

Dan promised that he will contact me as soon as he has something else suitable.

"You sound tired," he said as were signing off.

"It is hard going. But it's ok. It's all just a bit crazy at the moment at home and stuff, so I really need to keep working."

"I know. And I promise you are top of my list. Look I'm writing your name down now, right on the top – MAISY MALONE."

"That's cool. How about you? You must be rushed too. Have you moved in with Sadie yet?"

There was a pause. "No." Then another pause. "I've been putting it off, is that bad of me?"

"I guess you have to be sure of these things," I replied.

"Exactly! That's what I think."

"And are you sure it's what you want to do?"

"I'm not sure if I'm sure…" he laughed. "Oh God, I've got some crap to sort out."

"Everything works out in the end!" I told him with confidence.

"Does it, Maisy? Is that what you believe?"

"Of course I do. You have to, don't you?"

The thing is, I think I was trying to convince myself more than I was trying to convince Dan.


## Comments

**Popsicle:** You have to be positive, hun. Being negative will sap your soul…

Have you read my draft yet?

**Glen @LondonRiotCleanUp:** You're turning into an Agony Aunt

**MaisyM:** I don't think I'm a very good one!

Sorry Pops – I'm on it!

**Wednesday 5th October 2011**

**Alice**

I sat with Alice during our break today hoping to find out more about her. All these days of working together and she's still barely spoken to me. I get more conversation out of Dave.

Alice was sitting opposite me, sipping her black coffee and staring vaguely into the distance. She didn't look unhappy, but she certainly didn't seem very relaxed either. I've never really the noticed the tendons on someone's neck before, but Alice's are really prominent, like they are straining to pop out.

"Are you married?" I asked her. She didn't wear a ring, but lots of the girls there removed their jewellery before they started their shifts.

Alice just shook her head and carried on staring into space. The tendons were still bulging. I could imagine plucking them, like a guitar.

The small restaurant that we were sitting in was pretty empty, apart from another chambermaid in the far corner reading a magazine. There were no guests there then, as the lunch service wasn't active until twelve. It was quite a nice eating area, royal blue, with a thick plush carpet and they made a decent cup of tea. I wouldn't mind dining in there.

"I live with a man, have done for eight years. He has – problems. He's not worked for years."

I looked up, surprised, as I hadn't expected Alice to start talking. She wasn't looking at me and a small frown was forming on her pale face.

"My Dad hasn't worked for years either, not since my Mum walked out. He struggled to get work after losing the last job. Now he lives in the pub. Some days he doesn't even get dressed."

Alice shot me a look. "How is that the same? My Dean has MS. He can't work and he gets so angry about it. It all falls down to me. Every day is a struggle." She took a sip of coffee. "And do you know what; all I want to do most days is run away. Isn't that awful? What sort of person does that make me?"

"I don't know," I answered lamely. "An honest one?"

For the first time Alice smiled and it was a lovely smile. It actually lit up her whole face and made her look quite pretty, less drawn.

"Do you know what Maisy, there was one time when I thought I had the answer. I had the escape. Right here in this crummy hotel. There was this guy working in the kitchens, Pete, and we just clicked. I really didn't want anything to happen, but for once in so, so long I had found someone who made me laugh. Who wanted to hold me tight."

She paused and looked at me hard. "I'm not sure why I'm telling you this, you're just a young girl. But it's so hard."

"I might be young, but I see how unhappy you are."

"I had the chance. Pete wanted me to leave my husband. But I couldn't. What sort of woman walks out on a sick man? What sort of person would that make me?"

There wasn't much to say to that. I just touched her hand gently. She dipped her head and turned away, before suddenly shaking me away.

"Come on," she said. "Our break is over."

And as we were leaving the restaurant she turned to face me. "Maisy, be careful with your Dad, there may be more going on with him than you know. Sometimes we miss things in the people that are closest to us."


## Comments

**Lucy Locket:** Poor Alice, she has to leave. Life is too short to be so unhappy

**Popsicle:** But she feels loyalty towards her sick husband, I can understand that.

**Superstar3:** What an awful situation.


## Friday 7th October 2011

### Nanna Noo 2

I called Nanna today for our usual chat. She was quite perky considering she had a nasty cold; she sounded a bit like Darth Vader, except Darth Vader isn't as abusive.

"Bloody pain, I was going to clean my gutter today!" she complained. "I blame the bus; I'm always catching germs off the unhealthy prats on that. At least three people sneezed on me yesterday; one even left a trail of Wotsits behind on my best coat. Doesn't anyone cover their nose these days?"

"Nanna, you shouldn't be doing that at your age." (By *that* I meant the gutter, not the bus.)

"Why the hell not? The minute I stop is the minute I get old. And the minute I get old is the minute I scratch a hole for myself in the ground to curl up and DIE IN!" She paused to cough. "Besides, who else is going to do it for me? I can't see you leaping up to offer."

"Well, I'm not much good with heights…"

Last time I went up a ladder, I was trying to climb a tree house in Brian Shindon's garden. I got stuck halfway, frozen to the spot and had to be rescued by Brian's rather large and very grumpy father. I wasn't invited back.

"You've got no balls, my girl."

I didn't argue with this.

Nanna's language never fails to surprise me, but she worked for years at a pipe factory full of men. I'm not quite sure what her role was, but I know that she had to stand her ground early on in life. In later years she worked at a football club, serving tea and washing the kit, but I think to be honest she would have preferred to have been the manager (and would have probably done a better job of it).

"Talking about prats – is your dad still on strike?" she asked.

"Yes, he says so. But I think he is wavering. His best mate Norm has invited him to his 60th birthday bash in two weeks. He has to go to that. It's a free bar, he hasn't said he will go but I know he will."

"Of course he won't stick it out, he has no staying power. What about Ollie?"

"He's been out for a few evenings now. But I'm worried – Jess's been over and they've been flirting."

"Tell her to stay the hell away, he's no good for her, mark my words – I know these things." Nanna then erupted into another coughing fit. I thought it might be wise to change the subject.

"Have you spoken to Mum about the wedding?"

"Bloody daft if you ask me. They've only been together for five minutes. Would you believe she wants me to give her away?"

"And will you?"

"Well yes, I'm only too glad to get rid of the dappy mare."

"Oh Nanna," I suppressed a laugh. "Well if it makes you feel any better, I'm going to be bridesmaid and Ollie's going to be pageboy!"

"Pageboy? Bloody hell, it gets worse! Next you'll tell me your Dad is going to sing the first bloody hymn! It's all getting out of hand. Why can't they have a small little affair like a normal couple? And I hope that man of hers will get his hair cut at least. It looks like it's been dipped in a vat of bacon grease."

"He likes his long hair, Nanna. I just hope he can control the sweats."

"Loose clothing, that'll do the job. Maybe they should go the whole hog and put him in a bloody dress too." Nanna started coughing again, obviously getting herself worked up.

"I've got to go now, Maisy. I have some more hate letters to write to those money-grabbing, Tory bastards. If they think they can ignore me, they have another thing coming."

And with that she thumped down the phone.

My Nanna would make a useless MP. She's passionate enough, but she would end up pissing off half of parliament and frightening the rest.

But sometimes I wish I was more like her.


## Comments

**Glen @LondonRiotCleanup:** Can I contact your Nanna about a local demo? Does she have an email?

**MaisyM:** Seriously? Yes she does

**Glen @LondonRiotCleanup:** Yes, seriously. Get her to email on glen-riot-clean-up@mailbox.com

**007:** Go Nanna

**Friday 8th October 2011**

**Alone Again...**

Alice called in sick today. Monica wasn't impressed. She said that she 'detected a lie in her voice.' I'm not quite sure how a 'lie' can be detected, unless you have someone rigged up to a machine on Jeremy Kyle. I'm starting to think that all managers are suspicious and slightly neurotic.

However, Alice calling in meant that I had to work the shift alone today for the first time and it was pretty daunting. I've never had to do beds AND bogs! For the sake of meeting the deadline, I had to cut a few corners here and there, skimming over the shower a bit, not cleaning right into the corners, but I think the rooms looked OK. Also I got to choose what cable TV I listened to, so instead of Alice's love ballads I was able to listen to a bit of dance music.

I should give Alice a tip, dance music makes you move quicker. I'm sure I got the beds stripped at twice the speed. It doesn't have the same effect if you have Westlife wailing in your ear.

Monica was pleased with me and said that I had done a 'pretty good job considering.' I did notice her fingering the toilet roll in dismay. (I just couldn't be arsed to make that pointy shape thing at the end – I mean really, do people care about that sort of thing? Surely someone doesn't go to wipe their bum and then say aloud 'what a disgrace, this toilet roll is hanging freely, when it should be pointy like an arrow – I feel quite unable to use this on my bum now!')

Monica even said that she might be able to put in a good word with the BIG BOSS and try and get them to extend the work for at least another week.

When I got home, the place looked like a hell hole. I haven't really been doing much cleaning in the last few days, but I was half hoping that Dad and Ollie might pick up the slack. Sadly, neither of them have that mentality. Really, I wouldn't even mind if they just put their stuff in the washing machine, ready for me to turn on. Instead, a pile builds up on the floor beside it, spilling over into poor Dave's bed – I'm sure he doesn't want to sleep with festering socks and pants. And why can't either of them wash-up? Even simple things like half-finished mugs of tea are left to stagnate by the side of the sink.

"You need to wash me a top, love!" Dad yelled when I walked in. "I'm off out tonight."

"Oh yes, of course Dad. I've just been working a shift. It'll be no trouble at all to do your washing as well!"

"Now don't be moody, I thought you'd be pleased. I'm going back to the Pride."

"But what about your strike? What about your principals?" I asked.

"Screw my principals. I think I've made my point," he muttered, flapping his hand. "Anyway, according to Norm – that new landlady is alright!"

"I told you that the other day!"

"Yeah, well. It's another person agreeing with you. And now I can see for myself. Let the dog see the rabbit and all that…"

I reluctantly did Dad's washing, throwing a clean (but slightly damp) shirt at him when he came to leave. I was, however, pissed off to see Ollie still hanging around the house. My stomach filled with dread, thinking my evening of peace would be spoilt if I had to spend it with him.

"Aren't you going with Dad?" I asked hopefully

"Nah, not tonight," Ollie replied, looking all smug. "I've got a date with a lovely lady."

I didn't say a word, just slipped up to my room, stuck my music on high and flopped on my bed.

Instead of brooding, I have spent the last hour reading Poppy's Miss Stake – and do you know what, for a Vampire/love story thingy, it's not all that bad.

*My name is Holly Stake and I am a vampire. But the truth is, I cannot abide anything about my life in the darkness, I hate the taste of blood (even though I need it to keep me alive), I detest living in the shadows and more importantly I long to be part of another gang. I want to be a member of the Real Crew.*

*The Real Crew are cool – they are a gang with attitude and taste. They prowl the streets with a sense of purpose and authority. I so long to be part of them. To breathe their air, to be part of their scene.*

*But most of all I long to be with Riley.*


**Comments**

**Popsicle:** Yea!!! I'm so glad you like it

**MaisyM:** Real Crew? Sounds a bit like Melissa Henderson's lot?

**Popsicle:** Yeah, well, some of it is based on a little fact...

**MaisyM:** As long as you don't want to be part of their gang? I would be worried then!

**Popsicle:** Are you serious babe, I'm just using the idea. Guess what? I'm not a vampire either!

**MaisyM:** Lol – thats ok then x

**Lucy Locket:** I want to read it now too


**Saturday 9th October**

**Melissa's New Hair**

We were round Poppy's tonight, watching X Factor and trying to sing along. Jess reckons that she could be a singer if her boobs were a bit bigger. I'm not sure what her boobs have got to do with it, but her voice is enough to shatter eardrums (sorry babe – but you know it's true).

I prefer Strictly Come Dancing. I would love to learn to dance like that, all elegant and swirly, but Jess just laughs and says it's too 'posh' and 'naff' and Poppy is actually a bit scared of one of the judges.

But it was nice. Sitting together, jeering at the screen. Jess lying upside down on the bed and shouting abuse at the stupid sob stories. Poppy sitting all demurely and wiping away the odd tear (she's a sucker for a dead parent or dog or whatever).

"Everyone wants to be famous," Jess moaned. "What's wrong with settling with what you have? Being average?"

"Some of us want more," Poppy replied.

I saw her eyes flicker over to a pile of neatly stacked parcels. I knew these were her submissions of her book, ready to be farmed out to various literary agents.

"Yeah, well...it's just dreams babe. Sometimes it's best to stick in the reality." Jess muttered, squinting at the screen.

"Do you think that?" Poppy asked, looking directly at me. "Surely you want more?"

"I guess...But how likely is it that I'm going to get it? Really? The likes of me never achieve very much..."

"God, this is depressing," Jess groaned. She got up and stomped over to her computer. "Here you go; I'll show you something to make you laugh."

Bringing up her Facebook account, Jess searched and found Melissa Henderson's profile. There, for all of us to see, was her new and particularly tragic haircut.

"Oh dear," Poppy sighed. "That look does not suit her at all."

Melissa has quite a long, mean face anyway and the pixie cut that she had adopted just made her features look even more severe. That and the new, bright red colour.

"It's not just that; read her profile," Jess urged, pointing at the screen.

*He's dumped me. So gutted. Been crying all day...*

"Melissa. Hard nut Melissa?" I couldn't quite grasp this. "Melissa – who wanted to stamp on my face at school for wearing the wrong trainers – has been crying? I didn't know she was capable of emotion..."

Jess laughed. "I knew it would cheer you up."

"Well, it's made me see her in a new light."

Jess flopped back on the bed and focused her eyes back on the screen. "Sometimes there's stuff going on in people's head that you never know. We are screwed up in our own little ways."

### Comments

**Glen @LondonRiotCleanup:** Your mate is dead right. We are all screwed...

Glad your bully has had a bit of karma, but aren't you worried she'll read about herself on here

**MaisyM:** Do you think I'm crazy? I've changed her name. My life wouldn't be worth living if not!

**Glen@LondonRiotCleanup:** Wise move

**JesseBelle:** BTW I still do have a peek now and again. I do NOT break eardrums ;o)

**MaisyM:** Lol - sorry

## Tuesday 18th October 2011

## Room Service

I wasn't in a good mood when Dan called today. Everything had already gone wrong, so having the call from your Recruitment Agent to say that my last day was definitely next Saturday, was not a great end.

You see I had already missed my alarm, so I arrived at work five minutes late without a breakfast, to be told off by the delightfully polite but still fairly moody Monica.

The only good news was that Alice was back – but she looked pale and peaky and would not say much except to confirm that her fella, Lenny, had taken a turn for the worst.

"He has black moods," she said softly. "He can't sleep and he wants to talk and talk. I'm not sure I have the energy anymore."

The shift was particularly hard and for some reason my rooms seemed especially dirty. I'm not sure why people leave hotels in such a state. If I ever have money (ha, ha) I swear I will still tidy up after myself and not leave clumps of hair in the shower or nasty stains in the toilet.

So when Dan called and said that my job was going to end, I was already snappy.

"Ok," I said. "What will you have lined up for me next, I wonder?"

"Hard day?" he asked softly.

"You could say that. I think I might become a monk or something."

"You're the wrong sex, and anyway – what a waste," Dan replied. "Come in on Monday. I'll discuss the options with you then."

So that's what we agreed. And I walked home; still in a bad mood but smiling slightly that Dan thought I would be wasted in a monastery.

At least somebody seems to appreciate me.


## *Comments*

**Popsicle:** I appreciate you! Silly...

**007:** Things can only get better!

**Wednesday 19th October 2011**

**When Alice Met Nanna**

Alice was so depressed at work today; she barely ate her morning biscuit, just nibbled at it pathetically. She looked more drawn and pale than ever before.

"I don't want to go home after this shift," she admitted, finally. I was amazed that she was actually being forthcoming about something. "So what are you doing after?"

"Well, today I'm going to visit my Nanna. She likes the company to be honest. If she doesn't get to shout at me, the poor milkman will be subjected to it."

Alice looked disappointed. Immediately I realised that she needed to be away from her house for a bit.

"Come with me. Nanna loves meeting new people. Just be warned, she can be a cantankerous old cow."

Alice smiled and looked relieved. "I'd love to meet her," she said. "Thank you."

It was a bit odd taking Alice with me on the bus to Nanna's house. She still didn't speak much, just sat next to me clutching her small bag tightly on her lap. She seemed to somehow shrink into the seat itself.

"Was Lenny hard work again last night?" I asked.

Alice stared at me for a while before answering. "He's always hard work. But some days it's harder than others. The thing is I'm not sure I can do it much longer."

I was quite relieved when we reached the right stop and could take the short walk to Nanna's house. She was actually outside when we arrived, peering over her neighbour's hedge.

"What are you doing?" I whispered, worried that someone might see her.

"I'm sure that cow is having an affair!" she boomed back, obviously not concerned about keeping subtle. "She has the same young fella in every afternoon. And when she comes out she looks awfully guilty."

"Nanna, it may not be what you think."

"Oh, I'm sure it is." Nanna suddenly noticed Alice standing meekly behind me. "Don't mind me, dear, I'm just jealous. It's been years since anyone tended to my lilies – so to speak."

She took us into the house and put the kettle on, muttering about 'women's needs' and 'pent-up frustrations.' I was really beginning to regret coming when Alice suddenly chirped up.

"I hate my husband."

Nanna looked from her to me, and back again, patted Alice on the hand and said, "You need something stronger than tea, sweetie!"

Nanna only gets her brandy out if something important happens or someone dies (which is occurring more frequently in her world). She poured us both a small glass and herself a much larger one.

"Now then, I take it you have been married for some time?" she said, pushing up her pink glasses and peering at Alice intently.

"Yes," Alice replied. "To Lenny. We've been together for years but he's not well, hasn't been for a long time. He gets so depressed."

Nanna tutted. I was sitting there feeling like a spare part and Alice just looked awful, like she wanted to crawl off and die in a corner somewhere.

"I know it's bad, but I'm lonely; I just want to feel loved again," she moaned.

"Do you love him?" asked Nanna.

"No," Alice almost whispered. "I think I detest him. He shouts so much, like he blames me because his legs don't work and because he gets so tired. I feel sorry for him, but I don't love him."

"Then you have to leave him," Nanna said, and she knocked back her brandy.

"Are you sure?" I hissed at her. "She's all he's got."

"And there are people, professionals, that can help him," Nanna snapped back. "Why should Alice here, give up her life for a man she can no longer stand to be around. Life is far too short to live like that. It's not fair on either of them."

Alice started to cry and Nanna took her white, skinny hand in her yellow, mottled one.

"I'll tell you something my dear, something that I've not told anyone – not even gobby over there…" She nodded over at me and I immediately felt offended. "I lived a miserable life with my Johnny. For a start he farted continuously and never apologised, and he was such a moany, sulky, old sod. He would go days not speaking to me, just because I had burnt his fish or forgotten to iron his vest. We hated each other really, but we just put up with it, because we had little Barbara and because that's what you did in those days."

She paused to rub Alice's hand a little bit more, before continuing.

"One day I met a man at the football club. He was a referee, Willy Falmer. Lovely man with a beautiful, tight bum. Anyway, to cut to the chase, we had an affair and I fell in love. I was fifty two and planning to leave Johnny. But then what happened? Willy had a fatal heart attack on the golf course, died immediately at the 8th hole. I never saw him again. So me and Johnny just carried on as before and I guess because of the guilt I tried to make it better."

"But you always said you could never leave this place because your Johnny was here?" I said. "You must have loved him really?"

"Maybe I did. But we had a child together and we ended up getting used to each other, like a cat does with its fleas. For Alice it's different, the role has changed. She's no longer his lover or his friend. She's his unpaid nurse."

Alice got up then, kissed my Nanna delicately on the head and said, "I have to go now." And without another word she flew out of the door.

My Nanna looked at me and shook her head sadly.

"She knew it all already, Maz. She just needed somebody else to tell her."


## Comments

**Lucy Locket:** Thats so sad – poor Alice

**007:** There's nothing sadder than being with someone you don't love

**MaisyM:** You sound like you know

**007:** Maybe I do…

**MaisyM:** That must be hard??

**007:** It can be, especially if you are starting to like someone else.

**MaisyM:** I guess you have to do what you think is right

**007:** That's what I think too ;o)


**Thursday 20th October 2011**

**Poppy**

The shift at work was a bit awkward today. Alice still didn't talk much (no surprises there then) but she had a look of concentration that told me to leave her alone.

But as I was getting ready to go, she grabbed my arm and whispered. "I'm leaving him for Gary. I found his number last night and we talked for hours. It was like we'd never been apart. Thank your Nanna for me."

I wasn't sure whether to be pleased for her or not. I could imagine poor Lenny at home, all heartbroken and deserted, it seems wrong somehow. On the other hand, Nanna is right, life is too short…

There was no sign of Dad or Ollie when I got home. Dave was enjoying the freedom by sprawling out on the sofa, happily chewing on a pizza wrapper that he must have dug out of the bin. I fear his specialist diet could be hampered this week.

After a short nap and shower, I was only too glad to leave the house and go over to Poppy's. I had got a text from her this morning saying:

*Fright night needed. Come over asap*

Fright night means watching the crappiest film we can find in her Mum's extensive video collection (yes they still have a video player), most of which are straight to rental or 'made for TV.'

Tonight's choice was one of her Mum's most recent purchases – William and Kate.

"I thought it would be nice, seeing as we had such a lovely time watching the wedding," she gushed.

This was a lie, but I didn't want to upset her. We'd all watched the wedding at the Pride (Jimmy thinking it would be lucrative to have a themed party) and I had the embarrassment of my Dad shouting about 'Pippa's bum' and 'jiggling watermelons.' Most of the locals got too drunk by the end and there was a huge fight where Norm got pushed into the Royal Punch.

Poppy obviously felt that the film of William and Kate would be romantic, comforting and reminiscent of fairytales. It wasn't, it was cheesy, false and painful.

All the way through the film, Poppy looked tearful and stressed, she kept making weird gulping noises and then starting tugging at her hair. Towards the end, I grabbed her hand and asked her if she was okay.

"No," she gushed. "No, I'm really not. It's been an awful day."

She got up and walked towards the desk and came back with a fistful of sheets, which she thrust at me quite forcefully.

"Just a few weeks," she gasped. "And look, I've been rejected already."

The sheets of paper were various emails Poppy had printed off.

"These are rejections from my email submissions. I've only just sent out my postal ones." Poppy sniffed. "They obviously hate me. They obviously think I'm useless."

The emails were very polite and said very similar things - 'thank you for your submission'... 'I'm afraid I'm not the agent for you' ...'best of luck elsewhere.'

"They don't hate you, Poppy. It's just opinions. You have to keep trying."

"But Jess is right. It's just silly dreams. Dreams and fantasies. I was stupid for thinking I could be a writer."

I squeezed Poppy's hand and looked into her teary, blue eyes.

"Don't give up on them, Poppy, please. You're so lucky to have them. Please keep trying..."

"But I'm not sure..."

"Do it for me!"

I've never felt as angry and as passionate as I've felt about this. Poppy has to keep going. Because one of us has talent and it shouldn't be wasted.

I couldn't bare it if we all ended up getting nowhere.


**Comments**

**Lucy Locket:** You are good friend

**MaisyM:** Thank you

**Popsicle:** Yes, you are xx

And I will keep going – promise x

**MaisyM:** THANK YOU XXX

**007:** I think you are talented too

**MaisyM:** But you don't know me

**007:** I can just tell

**MaisyM:** Really?

**007:** Yes, trust me. Believe in yourself more x

**MaisyM:** Who are you 007?

**007:** ;o)


## Friday 21st October 2001

### Alice

It was my last day of work at the Grange, and you know what? I felt a little bit sad. I might even miss the little rooms and jiggling my bum to Bruno Mars while stripping the bed.

Then again, I won't miss the early starts, the relentless backache and the piss on the toilet seats.

Alice was sweet and brought me a little cake on our break. She looks different now, almost glowing.

"I told him," she said. "And I'm moving out tonight. He wasn't surprised. I think he was relieved. He said he knew I was resenting him."

"Will he be OK?"

"He has family. And I will still visit him, but as a friend now." Alice frowned slightly. "I'll miss you, Maz. You've only been here five minutes, but you've changed so much."

"You did it all by yourself," I reminded her. "You didn't need an idiot like me to help you."

"I know, but even so…"

"Even so, we can keep in touch."

"Yeah, but the reality is we won't. We move in completely different circles." Alice spoke matter-of-factly. "Although thank you for saying it."

I gave her a hug and my phone number anyway even though I doubt very much that'll I hear from her.

In a strange way I will really miss her though.

There have been anti-capitalist marches in London today, outside St Paul's. Nanna called to say she wanted to go, but she had to stay in to have her gas meter read.

Dad was watching the news and grumbling as usual.

"It's the bloody bankers that have done this to us. Can't trust the idiots that work for them."

I sometimes wonder whether Dad forgets that his own son was a banker once.

"I'm glad I've got no money," he told me earnestly. "It means that those greedy tossers can't get their grubby hands on it."

I find it all a bit depressing if I'm honest. All the news is about protests, marches and that Colonel Gadaffi getting shot in the head.

I'm doing the lottery tomorrow. You never know..!

## Comments

**Lucy Locket:** Good on Alice. I hope she's happy now

**Glen@LondonRiotCleanup:** Such a shame your Nanna couldn't make it today

**MaisyM:** You tried to get her to go?

**Glen @LondonRiotCleanup:** Yeah – emailed her last week. She's an inspiration!

## Saturday 29th October 2011

### Norm's party

I am writing this at midnight, after a night at the Pride for Norm's 60th.

I was disappointed to hear that Jess was going with Ollie, but hey? What could I do about it? Poppy agreed to come with me, so at least I wasn't Billy-no-mates.

Dad was very excited about the night out – he had a bath and everything. He came out smelling quite fragrant (because he'd used my expensive cocoa butter cream that Nanna had got me for my birthday) and his hair was all fluffy and fly-away.

"I used your coconut conditioner," he explained. "But I think I put too much on. My hair looks like a mad professor's now."

He must have used half a tub, because his thick grey hair was now quite "bouffant."

"Dad, did you use it on your eyebrows too?" I asked, looking closely at his strangely fluffy brow area.

"I used it on all my hairy parts!" Dad declared proudly.

I think that conditioner will be going in the bin.

I'm not sure why he was going to such an effort. I can only assume it's because Norm is one of his best mates and he will be glued to his side for most of the night. Maybe he's finally realised that the tramp look is not a particularly fetching one.

Norm and my Dad met years ago when they both used to play cricket for the local side. These were in the days when my Dad actually had a back (I do not remember these days well, he has always complained about his back at some point or another, even when he was working). Norm, apparently, was a fantastic spin bowler and my Dad was the leading batsman. They often talk about "silly points" and "googlies" and "mid-offs" – I think they make more sense when they're drunk.

At least I walked into the pub with a sweet smelling, fluffy Dad tonight.

Poppy had found us our usual seat in the corner, which I was pleased with as it had a good view of the karaoke machine.

Norm was already up there. He's quite a large man, with a worryingly red complexion that makes you wonder if his heart is going to pack up at any moment. Judging by the moves and thrusts he was making to Tom Jones, this could have been any time soon.

"It's a bit obscene, really," Poppy moaned, grimacing at Norm's gyrating pelvis, not helped by his broken flies.

"He's old. He's sad. Let him have his moment." I worried that it would soon be my Dad up there, doing his usual Mick Jagger impersonation.

I was surprised that for most of the early part of the evening, my Dad was leaning against the bar chatting to the landlady, Debs. She seemed to be commenting on his fluffy hair, as she kept touching it and laughing in her horsey style. My Dad seemed relaxed in her company and kept tossing his head back, like he was in a shampoo advert. If he wasn't so old and weird, I would have sworn blind he was flirting.

I tried to ignore him and concentrate more on my mate, who was jabbering on about her new lease of enthusiasm (six more submissions yesterday). I hope she gets something positive too or we will both suffer.

I felt bit depressed anyway. I could now see Jess and Ollie at the bar. They were standing very close and giggling. Jess looked over at us one time and waved, and then beckoned for us to come over. I ignored her.

"Why do you still hate him?" Poppy asked.

"He's a knob. And he's stringing her along. I know it!"

I then had to watch as Ollie performed a quite camp and annoyingly funny performance of Queen's 'I Want To Break Free' using 80-year old Jean Lennard's tartan shopping trolley as a hoover. Jean was shrieking with laughter and then started to join in, shaking her hips back and forth in a violent manner. She is one of the "old bunch" that always come on a weekend and sit by the window, sipping their Port and Lemon and harping on about the old days. Nanna can't bear them — she says they have their feet 'so firmly planted in the grave, they've taken root.'

Jean is also one of those women that have developed a weird shape. Their back and their bum almost become like one, there's just no indication of where the back ends and the arse begins. Believe me, it looks even weirder when they're rolling on the floor with their stubby legs scissoring in the air, alongside your gobby brother who suddenly thinks he's Freddie Mercury.

I wanted to get up and shout — "He's not funny. He's making that poor old cow make a right tit out of herself, we can see her beige knickers for God's sake! And surely a woman with a dodgy hip should not be swinging her leg over his shoulder like that! It's gross! He's just an attention seeker!"

In fact I could feel myself get more frustrated as the evening wore on. My Dad was now standing with his arm draped around Ollie's shoulder, crowing about his 'successful son.' Jess was standing with a smug grin on her face all evening, even Poppy walked over and started asking his advice on how best to invest her money. (I didn't even know she had any! And why was she asking someone who had managed to lose a load and refused to tell us how?)

I slipped out in the end, without anybody noticing. I had the echoes of Dad singing "Dancing in the Street" with Ollie, following me out.

As I'm sitting here now I feel so angry and I don't even know why. I don't even feel like I fit any more, in this weird family of mine. Ollie has come crashing back, and my position is being pushed out. I feel like a jigsaw piece that has lost its place.

I'm not really sure where I'm meant to go from here…

## Comments

**Popsicle:** Why did you leave? It was a good night? Ollie is so funny

**MaisyM:** I guess I wasn't in the mood

**Popsicle:** Shame – you missed a good one

**Sunday 30th October 2011**

**How to Wax a Sweaty Man.**

Ollie had a hangover today and was very quiet on the way to Mum's. To be fair, he did look really ill. He was walking really slowly, which is unlike him. Usually I get breathless just trying to keep in step. Today, we were almost crawling along.

"What time did you get home?" I asked him.

"Late…" he grunted, rubbing his temples. "Me and Dad stayed behind with Norm and Debs. Drank some shots…..urghh…..can't remember much, I think we were singing Beatles songs."

"That figures, Dad always sings Beatles when he's truly bladdered. Did he sing My Sister Lilly?"

"The Whore From Piccadilly? Ah, yes, I remember now. I think he woke a few neighbours up with that one…"

"What about Jess, did she stay?" I asked.

Ollie looked confused. "Eh, no. I can't remember when she went to be honest. It's all a bit hazy..."

I was a bit worried about this, but knowing Jess, she would have left when the attention was no longer on her. Jess is not one of those people who can sit quietly in the shadows and watch others milking the attention.

"You did an excellent Freddie Mercury last night," I said, and yes, there was a hint of sarcasm in there.

"Don't Maz, please," Ollie begged. His cheeks were red. He did look genuinely embarrassed. "I should stay off vodka, it always brings out the show-off in me!"

Once we were at Mum's, Ollie threw himself on the sofa next to Sweaty Keith and placed a cushion on his tummy.

"Not much dinner for me, Mum," he begged. "I was out with Dad last night and I'm feeling a bit delicate now."

"What did that Clive do to you?" Mum said in what can only be described as a very over the top, sickly voice, probably better reserved for babies or poorly kittens.

Mum looked a bit harassed herself. Her hair was scraped back off her face in a short ponytail and her make-up was fairly minimal for a change. She looked old and tired. She grabbed my hand and pulled me into the kitchen.

"Maisy," she whispered. "I'm worried."

"What about?" I replied, not that concerned. My Mum tends to worry about the most ridiculous things. She once rang me in the middle of the night because she was worried that her nails had stopped growing.

"I think I need to do something about Keith's problem, you know, before the wedding," she said, giving me a wink.

"Oh!"

Well, this I understood. I had noticed a stale, salty smell when walking into the flat and hadn't been sure if it was Sweaty Keith or Mum's gravy.

"Maybe you could see a doctor?" I suggested, trying to be helpful. "There's things they can do for excessive sweating. Or maybe it's his weight?"

"No!" Mum exclaimed, looking quite hurt. "I didn't mean his gland problem. He can't help that. Besides, I find that quite manly."

"Really? Do you?"

"Yes," she snapped, giving me a look that said 'don't go any further!' "The problem I need fixing is to do with his hair. He has hair on his chest, his back, his shoulders – and it's so thick and dark. It just won't go with the lovely smart suit I have planned for him."

"Hair on his shoulders? Thick and dark? Eurgh, Mum that's gross!"

*Oh God, why was my Mum marrying this man. He sounded worse than that Beast in the Disney film – at least that Beast could hold a tune and had a decent house. Also the singing teapot could come in handy.*

"I have these!" Mum said ignoring my disgust and flapping some wax strips in front of me. "I want to give them a try to see if they work. We are looking at early December for the wedding, now that's not far away."

"And why does this involve me?"

"After lunch, when Keith is napping, I want you and Ollie to help me do it."

I can't believe I agreed to it, but I did. I whispered the plan to Ollie just before we sat down for dinner. He tried to suppress a laugh, but agreed to do it.

Poor Sweaty Keith. After eating a whole plateful of dinner, followed by a huge slice of strawberry gateaux, he took his usual spot on the sofa and settled down for his mid-afternoon nap.

Mum gave the nod and on we pounced, lifting up his damp T-shirt to reveal his hairy, matted chest. I took one side and Ollie the other, we slapped on the strips – looked at each other in anticipation – and then Ollie gave me the nod when the time was up.

It was strangely satisfying to tear a huge chunk of hair away from his wet skin, leaving the huge red patch behind. What I wasn't expecting was the huge, girly scream that leapt from Sweaty Keith's mouth.

"AAAAARGH!"

Ollie stood up, hands on hips. "I'm sorry, mate," he said, flapping his hairy strip in Sweaty Keith's face. "But you really are one hairy gorilla!"

Ollie looked at me and we both wet ourselves laughing. Even on the way home, we were still giggling about the poor bloke's 'bear-like qualities.'

I hate to admit it, but Ollie was tolerable today.

## Comments

**007:** Ow! Poor Sweaty Keith. I bet he loves you now!

**MaisyM:** He has silky smooth skin now....

## Monday 31st October 2011

### Trick Or Treat

It was Jess' bright idea to go out Trick or Treating tonight. She decided that if we all dressed as sexy devils, we might be able to rustle up some extra money.

In theory, this wasn't such a bad idea and Jess was looking pretty good in her sparkly red hot pants (that were creeping up her bum). However, red isn't my best colour, it just makes me look paler than ever and the short skirt that Jess had found for me was slightly too big and kept slipping down my hips. As for Poppy, she was squeezed into a slinky scarlet number and was looking pretty saucy – but could barely walk because the dress was so tight. We were reduced to shuffling down the street.

And why does Halloween have to be on one of the coldest evenings. Walking around in skimpy clothes with a cold north-easterly breeze shooting up your nether regions is never a great feeling. I was feeling grumpy before we even began.

"We'll be lucky to get a stick of chewing gum," Poppy was muttering, as she shuffled along. She looked as if she'd had an accident in her pants.

"Stop complaining," replied Jess absently. But she wasn't really listening; she was too busy texting on her phone.

"Is that Ollie?" I asked.

Jessie looked up at me, a bit startled. "What, oh...yes." She threw the mobile back into her bag again.

Because it was obvious that we couldn't get very far dressed like we were, we decided to concentrate on the streets nearest the pub. "That way we can grab a drink straight after," Jessie reasoned.

It wasn't a great success if I'm honest. Most houses wouldn't open their doors or had big, bog-off signs saying 'NO TRICK OR TREATS HERE!' One sign on a small, unassuming house said simply 'trick me and you die' – I think that's taking things a little too far, but it certainly did the trick....

About twenty more houses simply slammed the door in our faces or wouldn't even answer, even though we could see TVs flickering inside. At one house we made a small child cry because we looked "too shiny" (that was probably my t-zone).

Our grand total was £4.23, plus a few Haribo sweets, two lollypops and a packet of fruity condoms.

I don't think I'll bother next year.

### Comments

**Glen @LondonRiotCleanup:** Aw, you should have come my way.

**MaisyM:** I'll remember next time!

**Popsicle:** My feet are still hurting...

**007:** Next time dress up as hoodies. That will really scare people...

Might get you arrested too though...

**MaisyM:** ;o) Nah, don't think I'll risk it.

### Tuesday 1st November 2011

### Back with Dan

I went to Recruit4You today as arranged. I was a little bit concerned, wondering what the hell Dan would have rustled up for me this time!

As usual, the beautiful but sulky receptionist greeted me with all the warmth of an Ekismo with frostbite.

"You again?" she tutted, drawing a long, red fingernail across her pouty mouth. "I'm guessing you're here for Dan?"

I looked behind her. For once the office was empty. Dan was alone at his desk eating a sandwich. He looked up and smiled.

"Maisy! Come on over!" he shouted

He shifted a load of papers onto the floor to make room for me. I swear his desk has got even worse since I last saw him.

"How come it's so quiet?" I asked, looking over at the two vacant desks.

"Well, Faith is out on a client visit, trying to win us some new business and Sadie…well, Sadie has left. I don't think she liked the sales side."

"Really? Aren't you upset about that?"

Dan pulled a face, sort of twisting his mouth to one side. "Not really. It wasn't always easy working with her, especially as her heart wasn't in it. She's got a job in a fashion house in Soho now, dead exciting. She doesn't stop going on about it to be honest."

"Oh," I said, trying not to reveal my jealous face. "So it's just you and the other girl, Faith, now?"

"Yes – and the boss, Neil, when he can be bothered to show his face. He usually pops in, makes some calls, tells us what our targets are and then goes off again." Dan paused. "But that does mean that there is a vacancy now, if you're interested?"

"No." I shook my head. "I'm not sure I could do all that phoning. And working to targets sounds a bit scary."

"Well, it's a pain sometimes but the commission is good. Think about it, Maisy. I get the feeling Neil would like you. You're bubbly and have balls."

I laughed. "My Nanna told me I didn't have any the other day. I wonder where they sprouted from?"

Dan shrugged. "Either way, I think you have them. And to be honest I think you are better than the temp job that I'm about to offer you."

"Which is?"

"Shelf-stacking at the pound shop – Pound4Pound. Maybe doing some cashier work. It's nothing exciting, I'm afraid. And it's only for a few weeks, perhaps longer."

"I'll do it."

"Right…ok. I'll print out the details for you. I think it will start next week, so you'll have some time off."

"Yeah, like I need that," I muttered. "I need money, not breaks."

Dan started tapping away at his computer, my eyes scanned his desk, the several CV's lying there, the discarded application forms, his cold cup of tea. The mug said "best boyfriend" on it in lurid pink writing.

"Aw, did Sadie buy you that?" I asked.

Dan smiled, going a bit red and nodded.

"Sadie sounds a bit like a dog's name, don't you think," I said – and then regretted it (I always put my foot in my mouth).

I thought he would tell me off, but instead he leaned in forward and whispered, "I always thought the same."

I'm not sure why he whispered. Maybe he thought she had bugged his desk.

"Have you moved in yet?" I asked (I couldn't help myself).

"No." He stopped typing, his fingers pausing in mid-air, as if he was in the middle of a piano recital. "It's complicated, you see…"

Dan turned and looked at me directly. I had never really appreciated how very light blue his eyes were. They reminded me of little boy's eyes – quite cute.

"I'm not even sure I'm ready to move in yet. Sadie is so, well, demanding. And….Oh god this will sound so lame…"

"What will?"

"I will miss my dog so much. You see, I have a dog at my parent's house, Billy, and he means the world to me. But Sadie hates dogs."

"She hates dogs? How can anyone hate a dog? Mine poos all over my landing, but I still love him – somehow!"

"Sadie is just Sadie. She has her ways."

"Sounds like a cow to me, perhaps I was right about her name…" I stopped myself. "Sorry Dan, that was out of order. I'm sure she's lovely really. I've just never been able to trust anyone that doesn't like animals."

Dan smiled and handed me my printed assignment.

"Let's just put it this way," he said. "I'm not rushing into anything. But I think she is getting a little fed up."

I grimaced at him. "Good luck with that."


## Comments

**Popsicle:** Working at Pound4Pound, that's OK, but not really what you're after? You should have taken the agency job, you could do that.

**MaisyM:** I've never done anything like that before though. I think he was just being nice

**007:** You should give it go. What have you got to lose? If he thinks you can do it, he must see something?

**MaisyM:** I'll think about it...

**Lucy Locket:** Be confident, hun. You're better than you think

I'm applying for some new office jobs – hoping I won't be waiting tables much longer

**MaisyM@:** Keep me posted x


## Thursday 3rd November 2011

### Hanging on the telephone...

Dan called, quite early while I was still eating my toast.

"It's confirmed," he said, all chirpy. "You start on Monday."

"At the pound place? The one in the High Street?"

"Pound4Pound. Yes. Don't be late. We had loads of applicants for this one."

"Really?" I was surprised.

"Maz, do you know how bad things are at the moment? I'm getting professional people begging me for work at the moment. Just be thankful you have something." Dan sounded a little short.

"I'm sorry. I didn't mean to sound ungrateful. I'm just having a bad week. I really do appreciate all you've done for me."

"Good, because believe me I am pushing you to the top of the pile at the moment."

"Why?" I asked, tracing the crumbs round my plate. "Why are you doing that for me?"

"Because I like you…..Maisy, I'm sorry, my next appointment has come in. I have to go."

I was left feeling a little happier. Silly I know, but knowing that somebody, somewhere, has put you on the top of their pile makes all the difference to your week, even if the top of the pile is shelf stacking.

Not that there is anything wrong with shelf stacking, or being a chambermaid for that matter. I'm just not sure it was the direction I had in mind when I was still at school. Then I was still dreaming about an English degree, toying with the idea of journalism or perhaps teaching. Mind you, from the ages of five to about nine, I was convinced I was going to be an ice cream man. (Well, obviously not the 'man' bit, but somehow ice cream woman just never sounded right!)

I planned an early night tonight because I was still feeling a bit rubbish. I didn't expect to find Ollie crouched on the stairs, muttering into his mobile phone. He didn't see me and instinctively I went to move back into the living room, assuming that he was talking to Jess. But then I heard him say: "I miss you so much. It's a mistake me being down here. I should be back with you."

I bit my lip and immediately felt uncomfortable. OK, I should have walked away. But he was obviously talking to Lottie behind Jess's back. Wasn't it my responsibility, as her mate, to find out what was going on?

So, I crouched down in the dark hall and continued to listen.

"I know….I will, I promise. I think I'll come back up soon," he was saying softly.

My heart was thudding, it was so bloody loud I was convinced he would hear it, but you can hardly disguise a heartbeat.

"Of course – you know I love you. I hate all of this crap, I just want it to be over…"

*Oh, god*

"I miss you too…."

*Jesus, was he actually crying?*

"I will, I promise," he whispered. "Love you. Bye."

I'd never heard my brother cry before, not like this anyway. I'd seen him shed a few tears at Lion King once when he thought I wasn't looking, but nothing like this. I felt frozen to the spot, shocked and feeling quite emotional to hear him so upset.

I waited and listened as he moved up the stairs and heard the soft thud of his door close. I wondered if he would lie on his bed and continue to cry. Even though I was annoyed that he was messing Jess around, another part of me wanted to go upstairs and hug him, tell him it would be alright, that all relationships were worth fighting for – surely? For the first time ever, I think, I felt empathy for Ollie.

I sat there for a moment taking this in.

My moment of reflection was ruined however, when Dad stumbled over me, en route to the bathroom.

"What the hell are you doing, crouching down there in the dark for?" he yelled, rubbing the shin that he managed to bash against the radiator. "You look like a knobhead!"

I ignored his spluttering and went up to bed as planned. I did hover briefly outside Ollie's door and wondered if I should knock. But what the hell would I say? I was listening in on your conversation? This is what I think you should do?

I guess I have to let him make his own decisions and just hope that I can help Jess make some of her own. I'm assuming Jess still isn't reading my blog (she swore she couldn't be bothered with it any more). If you have read this Jess, I'm sorry.

But if not, I'm meeting her tomorrow night. Do I tell her?


## Comments

**Lucy Locket:** Yes – deserves to know

**Popsicle:** Oh, Maisy – are you sure you have all the facts right. If so, yes, tell her.

**007:** Be careful. Sometimes people don't like to hear the truth

**Glen @LondonRiotCleanUp:** Tell her.

**Friday 4th November 2011**

**Yeats Date**

Me and Jess walked together to the Pride and I was worried that I would let something slip about Ollie last night, but luckily Jess was leading the conversation and I didn't have to say much. Also lucky for me was the fact that I had barely seen Ollie all day, as he had been up earlier than me again. Dad said he is 'making plans.' I suspect these plans will involve London and a certain Charlotte.

My only concern was that Jess hadn't got too attached to him.

We entered the Pride and Jess immediately strolled up to the crowded bar and thrust herself forward. She's wasted in retail, really – she should be a glamour model or something more 'in your face.'

We then settled in our usual place in the corner.

"Are you meeting up with Ollie after this?" I asked her.

"No. He's doing something tonight. He was a bit vague, actually." She frowned and gulped back some of her drink. "I'm sure he's still got a lot on his mind, what with losing his job and all that."

"Yeah, I guess…"

"He's a good bloke, Maisy, honest. You have to learn to give him a chance. He's told me how sad he is that you're not closer."

"He's said that?" I shook my head. "He was probably just telling you what he thought you wanted to hear."

"Oh behave," she looked genuinely annoyed. "Why would I care really? If I fancy a bloke, it makes no odds to me whether he gets on with his sister, although obviously I would prefer it if you two did get along. For your sake as much as anything."

"My sake?"

"You can't keep blaming him for not being there, Maz. He had his reasons for leaving and I know it was crap that he didn't keep in touch, but he does love you. He loves all of you, even your crazy Dad!"

"He said this?"

"Yes. He told me that he finds it hard to fit in, that he loves his family but he doesn't really know them."

My stomach twisted, this sounded so familiar. Maybe we were more alike than I had realised.

"Just give him a chance, Maz," Jess said softly.

"How are you finding things with him?" I asked. I couldn't help myself.

Jess didn't answer at first; she was playing with a strand of her hair and staring hard at Poppy and Charlie (who were now leant in very closely together).

"We get on so well – he's so funny," she said finally. But I sensed a '*but*' coming. "But that's it really. There's no spark."

"Oh, OK."

"I am thinking he might want to take things slow, but I'm not feeling the passion. I'm just not sure *I'm doing it* for him – if you get my drift?"

I could tell this was hard for Jess to admit. I looked at her face, her lovely open, honest face and I knew then that I had to tell her my fears, even though I wasn't sure of all the facts.

"Hun, I've got a feeling he might still be hung up on his ex, Lottie." I ended up just blurting it out – with hindsight I wish I had been a bit more tactful. Poppy has always been better at these sort of things.

"Eh? What are you on about?"

"Ollie. I heard him on the phone, he was saying all this soppy stuff to someone. That he missed them. And that he wanted to be back with them."

"No…Ollie wouldn't go back to her. He told me all about her, she was a bitch. You must have heard wrong."

"I didn't, I –

Jess was shaking her head, her face looked odd.

"I'm sorry Maisy, this isn't right, talking about him like this. Something has obviously happened, something's not right. I need to talk to him myself."

And with that, Jess swept up her coat and raced out of the pub. She even left her drink untouched, which is unheard of.

As I waited for the bus home, I looked up at the sky and watched blooms of fireworks light up the night. Such beauty and sparkle, but gone in seconds.

To be honest, I hate fireworks. They're just another bloody letdown.

**Comments**

**Popsicle:** Oh no – didn't go well then?

Is Ollie home?

**MaisyM:** No, not yet

**007:** Don't panic. Let them talk.

**Saturday 5th November 2011**

**Nobody Loves Me**

Another 'not so great' day.

Ollie burst into my room this morning and demanded to know why I had been interfering with his life. I asked him what he meant and he then told me to 'keep my nose out' regarding him and Jess.

"We're just having fun, that's all, nothing heavy!" he spat. "It doesn't need any involvement from you, thank you very much."

"And what about Lottie? Are you still seeing her?"

"Lottie is nothing to do with you. It's over. Just keep out of my business."

And he stormed out of my room again.

I later got a text from Jess:

*I talked 2 Ollie and he said there's nothing goin on with him and Lottie. He seems really wound up bout something tho. I think u need 2 sort things out with him asap.*

And just when I thought things couldn't get any worse, Dad shouted at me for 'unsettling the harmonies of the house.' (He's a fine one to talk!)

"We were all getting along fine and then you start poking your nose in. Why can't you learn to get along with your brother?" Dad moaned on his way out to the Pride. "If you carry on like this, he'll be off again and we won't see him again for another six years. In six years I could be dead, remember."

I think this house is going crazy. In fact I think the world has gone crazy.

I'm even starting to wonder if I imagined the whole 'telephone call'- but then I look back on my blog that night and know that couldn't be possible. It happened alright, even though I wish it hadn't.

So I'm sitting here now, alone in my room apart from the neurotic dog, who is laying trembling under the bed as more fireworks explode outside our house (even Doris next door let off a couple of bangers).

I don't think this will do his nervous bowel much good.


## Comments

**Glen @LondonRiotCleanUp:** Aw Maisy I feel bad for you. Do you fancy coming to the big firework display at the Park? It might cheer you up?

**MaisyM:** No thanks Glen – think it's a night in for me

**Popsicle:** Don't panic babe. It'll be ok. Think Jess is fine about it

**MaisyM:** Ollie was right – I shouldn't have interfered

**007:** You did what you thought was best.

Don't beat yourself up about it.

**MaisyM:** Thank you, but I can't help feeling I made things so much worse

**007:** You didn't. Stop worrying

**MaisyM:** You're always so nice to me

**007:** I like being nice to nice people

**MaisyM:** Aw! blushing now


## Sunday 6th November 2011

### Dad Dismayed

I spent most of today lounging round the house feeling sorry for myself. Ollie was there, but ignoring me. It was pretty awkward to be honest.

Dad came home early from his lunchtime drink at the Pride because he got into an argument with some "Tory Tosspot."

It all started apparently when Dad was ranting about charity hand-outs being given to the poorer households.

"Over 30,000 people a day are relying on charity hand outs now!" my Dad was ranting. "Probably be us next if Maz can't hold down a job, I know they'll keep squeezing my benefits as much as they can."

Apparently this bloke then turned to my Dad and asked him what he was complaining about, as "no-one had actually died yet."

"What, just because no-one has died of starvation doesn't mean we're not screwing things up!" Dad had yelled back. "This amount of people should not be relying on charity to eat!"

Dad said he came close to hitting the smug so-and-so, but stopped when Debs intervened.

"I can't fight when there is a nice pair of breasts in front of me," he said slyly. I think this was directed at Ollie who was also in the room, but he was too busy texting on his phone to listen.

------

Came back to my blog just before bed. I heard the door slam half an hour ago and assuming it was Dad sneaking out, I went downstairs. But Dad was sitting there watching some dodgy film.

"He's gone again," he said to me, without looking away from the TV. He looked all matter-of-fact about it. "Took his rucksack and buggered off back to London."

"Ollie?" I asked (stupidly).

"Of course, Ollie. Who the hell else am I talking about? The bloody dog – although if that mutt took off it would be a blessed relief…"

"What did he say?"

"Not much. He was fiddling with that phone of his all night and then he said, 'I'm sorry, there's stuff I have to sort out,' and he's gone back. I bet that will be another six years before we see him again."

"Dad?" I stepped forward. Dad hadn't moved from the TV, but there was something in his body language that told me something wasn't right.

"I'm OK, Maisy. You go up to bed now. I'm OK."

I left him down there, sitting in front of that crap film and I know he stayed there all night. I also know he was crying.

## Comments

**007:** Maisy, I'm really sorry

**MaisyM:** What makes it worse is that this is all my fault

## Monday 7th November 2011

### Text Mystery

Jess texted me today

*Sorry 2 hear about Ollie, Poppy told me he's gone again. Hope you're ok.*

I replied:

*Think so. But are you? And are we ok?*

I had to wait twenty BLOODY minutes for the reply and then she said.

*I think so... But we need to talk soon. Stuff has happened*

So of course I then said

*Call me!!*

And then I got this reply

*I will...soon. Pls wait x*

This is not like Jess, at all. I don't like 'not knowing' stuff, so I tried calling her anyway, but her phone was switched off. There's no point trying her landline as Stella Bridges never paid the bill so it was cut off months ago.

I'm worried, but I guess I will have to wait.

I don't think it takes a genius to work out that Ollie has dumped her.

I just don't know why she can't tell me that.

## Comments

**Popsicle:** Hope she's ok. She's not answered my texts either.

**Lucy Locket:** Maybe it's for the best, Ollie being away for a bit. Give both you and Jess time to recover.

**MaisyM:** True, but my Dad is gutted. Haven't dared to tell my Mum yet...

## Monday 14th November 2011

### Pound4Pound

I thought Dad might wish me luck on my way to start my new job, but he was too busy reading a leaflet that been stuffed through the door.

"Would you believe this? They are only going to stick a bloody water meter outside our house. We have no choice in the matter either. That's it now, no more baths for me!"

"You rarely have them anyway," I replied.

"Well from now on we'll have to share our bath water." Seeing my look of disgust, he continued. "Or, I'll get a water butt and wash my bits in that. If the birds can do it, so can I."

I left work with that lovely image firmly planted in my head.

I've been in Pound4Pound a few times myself. It's one of about four pound shops in the centre of town. I often wonder what will happen with current inflation and whether they will suddenly be forced to become £1.25 shops. Either that or the stuff will become really, really crappy – like tea-bags with only a few specks of tea in them or leaky watering cans.

I went into the main entrance and wandered over to a rather large lady on the main till. She seemed to be oozing over the counter itself, like a model made out of Play-Doh. She had a lovely, warm smile with a large gap between her front teeth.

"I'm the temp," I said. "I'm not sure who I need to report to?"

"Oh," she said. Her voice was really soft and sweet. "That'll be Leon, the manager. I'll buzz him for you."

She reached below her counter, and wriggled her arm awkwardly about. Her face contorted into a weird shape while she did it, like she was struggling to find the button.

I was surprised, though, when Leon emerged from what I assumed was the back room. He was very small and scrawny, with long brown hair, parted centrally into 'curtains,' resting on either side of his rounded glasses. He also had a weirdly-shaped, wispy goatee that was trimmed into an inverted triangle – failing to disguise the adolescent acne on his chin. I never get those trimmed beardy things – they're neither one thing nor the other. To my mind, you either grow a full Father Christmas beard or you don't bother. It makes no sense to have a halfway house.

Leon smiled and half waved at me.

"You must be Maisy," he said. I liked him immediately for having a nice friendly smile.

I followed him as he showed me around the vast stockroom, full of every item you could imagine, knickers, sweets, bird feeders. There was even a special aisle dedicated to Christmas stock.

"Be careful of those boxes," he said, pointing at a particular shelf. "One nudge and you get a hundred gnomes singing 'White Christmas' – badly."

After a quick tour, Leon showed me around the store itself. I noticed that festive music was already being piped through the speakers.

"Doesn't that irritate you?" I asked him.

"You get used to it," he admitted. But he looked very sad about it. I could see the pain behind his small, rimless glasses.

He introduced me to the other staff members working that day. Wendy was the woman I met on the cash till. There was Sophie who was twenty two and very pretty and also mainly worked on the tills. Pete and Jed who mainly stayed in the stock room, they were in their thirties I would guess. Both had shaven heads, but Pete was skinny and Jed was very muscular. They both spoke in mainly grunts and 'alright darlins' but seemed harmless enough.

Last of all there was Ruby. Ruby was in her late forties – she was very stern looking with glasses and a strange, down-turned mouth which was accentuated by her descending cheeks. I'm not sure which area she worked in. I assumed she floats about and works where she wants. I get the feeling Leon is a little scared of her as he avoids her like the plague.

Later, when I was given the short tour of the small and very cluttered staff room I noticed a bowl of fruit on the table, with a note stuck on it stating 'Ruby's - Keep Off'. Therefore, I am assuming she is not a particularly friendly woman.

"We need someone mainly to replenish the shelves and cover the tills," Leon explained in his soft manner. "It should be easy enough work for you."

And, to be frank, the first day was. I was going back and forth a fair bit, filling up where needed. I also answered customer questions where I could. I was a bit nervous about being able to help the customers at first – as I was only temp, I assumed I wouldn't have the answers yet. This was until I realised most of them asked the same bloody question.

"How much is this?"

One woman became quite irate with me when she stuck a dog bowl under my nose, and demanded to know the price.

"It's a pound, Madam."

"But how am I meant to know that? There's no price tag on it. I'm not psychic, you know. You should make these things clearer."

"But this is a Pound Shop? It says 'everything a pound' on the door and on those big signs above your head? The ones in bright yellow?"

*The ones that nearly knocks you out because they are hung so low.*

The woman looked up and studied these signs for a while, before sighing and marching off with the dog bowl clasped to her chest.

"But you still shouldn't assume!" she shouted back at me in a haughty manner.

I learnt pretty quickly that as soon as someone came up to me, clutching an item in their clammy hands, with a puzzled look on their face, nine times out of ten they wanted to know the price.

It was a good day, though, and I liked the team – especially Leon who kept checking to see if I was alright. He was obviously a bit nervy and didn't like giving me orders, and actually that was a refreshing change.

I walked home feeling quite content. Quite relaxed even.

That was, until I checked my phone and saw that I had a text from Jess waiting for me.

*I'm pregnant*

## Comments

**007:** Oh. Bloody hell. Do you think its Ollie's?

**MaisyM:** I hope not... I just don't know...

**Popsicle:** Aargh? Really is that what she said? I'm texting her now!!

**Lucy Locket:** Poor Jess

## Wednesday 16th November 2011

## Jess Confess

Today I arranged to meet Jess after work. I didn't want her coming to the house because the place looks like a right state (I haven't had much chance to clean) and I didn't want to go to the Pride as I knew Dad would be there, mooning over Debs. Dad is practically living there now, especially now that Ollie has left. The few times I see him, he mutters about the 'disappointment of children' and the 'heartache of life' – so I assume he is in his dramatic stage, which comes before the anger.

I haven't even dared to tell Mum that Ollie has gone. When she calls I just make out that he's out or in the bath (she must think he's either really sociable or super clean). After all, how the hell will she take the news that her golden boy will not be at her big day? Thank God she can't be arsed to read my blog! I only hope that Ollie sorts out his issues with Lottie and then finds his conscience and comes back for the wedding. Perhaps he could bring the elusive Lottie with him?

I was a bit anxious about meeting Jess, because I wasn't sure how she was taking the news either.

Jess met me outside the door. She looked really pale and was dressed casually in tracksuit bottoms and a big, shapeless jumper. We decided to walk over the road to a small café.

"Do you want a tea?" I asked her.

"Nah, it makes me feel sick. In fact most things are making me feel dog rough at the moment. I'll have a hot chocolate."

We picked a booth at the back of the cafe and sat huddled together. The place was bloody freezing.

"I'm sorry I didn't tell you sooner," Jess said. "I was still deciding what to do."

"And what are you going to do?"

"Keep it," she said firmly. I already knew the answer. I've known Jess since we were five, there was no way she would do anything else.

"Aren't you going to ask whose it is?" she said.

"Only if you want to tell me," I replied.

"It's Steve's," she said, flatly. "I've been seeing him on and off all the time, but I'm about five weeks gone."

I couldn't help feeling relieved.

"Still early days, then?"

She shrugged. "I guess."

"So you were seeing him while you were with Ollie?"

"Yeah...I'm sorry. But Ollie knows now. I told him the other Saturday. There was no spark with us. We just liked chatting and drinking. I guess I just wanted to make Steve jealous."

"What about Ollie?"

"Ollie was just lonely. We wanted company, somebody to have a laugh with. He's still hung up on someone else and I kind of knew that, but we were happy to use each other."

"See! I told you, it's that bloody Lottie," I replied angrily. "Why did he deny it to me? He should've just admitted he was still upset about her."

Jess shook her head at me. "Maz, I'm not so sure it's her. He had a big argument on the phone once and it wasn't her name he said....And he was really upset afterwards...Oh Maz, you really need to talk to him, he has so much crap going on and he needs to talk to someone." She paused. "When you talked to me at the weekend, I knew I had to speak to Ollie face-to-face and find out what was going on with him. He knew I was still seeing Steve, but he wouldn't tell me who he was obsessed with. I couldn't understand why he wouldn't be honest with me, I thought we were mates."

"So why doesn't he talk to me? It's not like I haven't been around."

"Because he knows you blame him for walking out? I don't know…" Jess started picking her fingernails. "Families are screwed up."

"Tell me about it. And now he's gone back to London, just like I predicted. He didn't even think to tell me. Dad is upset, thinks it will be last we will see of him for years again."

Jess sat back in her chair and pushed back a long strand of hair that was falling into her face. "Nah. I reckon he'll be back this time. He knows how much the wedding means to your Mum. You just have to give him some space to sort things out. Like I said, I think things are more complicated then you think…"

"Why do you say that?" I was getting frustrated; was Jess keeping something from me.

"I don't know," Jess replied wearily. "It's just a feeling I get. It's up to you whether you believe it or not…I'm not being funny, but I have enough mess of my own to worry about at the moment without worrying about your family too."

She sat back in her seat, biting her lip hard.

"I'm sorry, Jess, this is meant to be about you, not Ollie." I paused, feeling awkward. "So, is Steve going to support you?"

"Yeah, he says so. He's all excited at the moment, but the reality's not kicked in. He thinks it's all about trips to the park and playing with toy cars, not pooey nappies and sleepless nights." She sighed. "That's why I need to know I've got your support if I need it."

"Of course you have, you don't even have to ask that."

I squeezed her hand and she closed her eyes. "I'm really scared, Maisy," she whispered.

"It'll all be OK, Jess, I promise," I said. "I'll help you through it."

"Thank you." She opened her eyes and faced me. "But you have to help your brother first."

## Comments

**Popsicle:** I'm so glad you guys have sorted it out. I'm seeing Jess tomorrow, she's knows she has my support too

**007:** I'm worried about your brother. He obviously never meant to mess Jess about. You should cut him some slack next time you see him

**MaisyM:** I think maybe I got a lot of things wrong

## Friday 18th November 2011

### Agent Dan

I left work at five as usual and popped to the Co-op on the way home to pick up some essentials. I find I'm buying less and less now. I can survive on a sandwich at lunch and some cheap pasta in the evening. Dad is rarely in. He has been in the Pride so often, Debs has got him changing the barrels and all sorts. I asked him how this was affecting his dodgy back, but he just muttered something about 'helping a beautiful woman out' and 'pushing the pain aside for others in need.'

I think the daft idiot is besotted.

And of course having Ollie doing his disappearing act has meant that I haven't needed to feed him either. Strangely I do miss him, which I wasn't expecting. Even though most of the time he was either texting, talking on his phone, or tucked away in his bedroom. He was another face, somebody else to greet on the landing. Somebody else to say goodnight to before I go to bed.

As I was standing in the bread aisle, squeezing the loaves to try and find the freshest option, Dan called to see how the latest assignment is going.

"It's not so bad," I told him. "But I'm still hoping I won't be there too long…"

I was thinking back to earlier this morning, when Jed kept squeezing past me in the stockroom, deliberately pressing his sweaty body next to mine. Or that time a little later in the afternoon, when I found his hand lingering a little too long on my bum. Why am I always too polite to say anything? I should tell Leon, but I'm not really sure Leon has the ability or the courage to tackle Jed.

"No, it won't be a long one; they were only looking for some cover for a few weeks," Dan replied. I heard a slurp and assumed he was drinking his coffee as he spoke to me. Either that or his dog was joining us in the conversation. "The feedback is great though. Leon really likes you."

"Cool, I like him too." There was nothing not to like, I just wish he was a bit more...well, like a boss I guess!

"By the way, we won't be using MJ Design again. You were right about them. They are now being investigated for many things; allegedly VAT fraud is amongst them."

"Really? How did you find that out?" I couldn't stop the beam spreading across my face.

"I shouldn't really be telling you this...but as we're mates...A young girl called Becca came into register last week. She said she had worked with you. Apparently she shopped them in to the authorities. Finally snapped when that Sheila told her off for having one cup of tea too many...."

I gasped. "Little, quiet Becca? Good on her. That's the best news I've heard all week."

"I'm glad I've been the one to deliver it to you," he paused. "Maisy, I was talking to my boss, Neil, about you again. I still think you might be suited to a job here."

"But why would you think that? I've never done recruitment in my life?"

"It's hardly rocket science. You just need to be good at talking to people, good at influencing them and I think you will be." He coughed. "Recruitment is sales, and sales is all about the gift of the gab. You strike me as someone gifted in that area – if you don't mind me saying."

"Really?" I wasn't sure whether to be flattered or not.

"Really." He was laughing. "You have to have more confidence in yourself, Maisy, you have to believe you can do these things. You are wasted in a Pound Shop."

I stood there clutching my overly squeezed and oddly shaped bread and wondered whether Dan could be right, whether I could actually make a go of recruitment.

"I could try and get you an interview with Neil for next week, what do you think?" Dan was saying.

What I was thinking was – Jesus! An interview? A proper, grown-up interview! What the hell would I wear? How would I know the answers to the questions? How could I not screw this up?

What I said was – "OK Dan, let's go for it."

I'm starting to feel a bit sick again.

## Comments

**Lucy Locket:** Yes!! Go girl. I've had 15 interviews so far, hope you're more successful than me!

**MaisyM:** 15 – bloody hell...

**007:** You'll be fab! Good luck.

**MaisyM:** Thank you

**Glen @LondonRiotCleanUp:** If not you can always join us at our next 'sit-in' protest....Think your Nanna might be there!!

## Saturday 19th November 2011

## OH GOD!!!!

I've been in A&E all night with Dad.

Long night and I'm very, very tired now (was there until gone nine in the morning). Will post a longer blog tomorrow....

## Comments

**Popsicle:** Hey – hope all is ok – texting now

**JesseBelle:** Babe – I'm worried now. Will text too

**007:** Hope all ok....Worried ;o(

**Lucy Locket:** Me too

**SuperStar2:** And me

**Glen@ LondonRiotCleanup:** And me!!

**SkySpotter22:** ...and me!!!

## Sunday 20th November 2011

### Humpty Dumpty

I can't believe the events of yesterday. I couldn't face blogging again. I needed to catch up on sleep and I also needed to look after Dad.

Nobody is sure of the specifics of why Dad was on the wall outside the Pride on Friday night. Norm, who had been standing with him, had his back turned at the crucial moment.

"I think," Norm had said, while we were waiting for the ambulance to arrive (I had had to leg it over after getting his frantic call), "that he was trying to demonstrate his athletic abilities by walking like a tightrope walker. We had been arguing about who was the most nimble footed. Of course it was a pointless discussion as I had been the fastest on the cricket pitch in our day. They hadn't called me Nifty Norm for nothing. Your Dad was insisting that he had the balance of an angel, which I disputed…"

It seemed a pretty pointless argument now that Dad was sprawled on the ground, with a puddle of blood forming behind his head. His eyes were open and he was moaning softly. Amazingly, he was still clutching his unscathed pint glass.

Debs, the new landlady, was crouched next to him, stroking his forehead and muttering softly into his ear. She looked up when I approached.

"Don't worry, love," she said sweetly. "I used to be a nurse. These things always look worse than they are. Your Dad is a tough old stick, he *will* be just fine."

He didn't look fine, lying there looking all weird and pale. Everything happened so quickly, it's a bit of a haze, really. The ambulance arrived, and two burly paramedics bundled Dad in. I was told to follow on behind. I remember standing there feeling utterly useless and hating myself for not being able to drive, before Debs grabbed me with her ring encrusted hand and told me she'd take us in her battered mini.

Debs didn't stop talking in the car. She kept gassing on about how much she liked the pub and what a lovely bloke our dad was, how he made her laugh with his wisecracks. She kept bouncing up and down on her seat as she drove and even though she was still wearing her high heels, her feet still barely reached the pedals.

Once at the hospital, Debs pulled right outside. "I'll leave you here as I'd best get back to the pub," she said. "But I will call later to see how he is."

It wasn't until later when I realised I hadn't given her our number.

I hate hospitals. Most people go on about the smell, but that doesn't bother me. Why would the smell of disinfectant upset anybody? No, for me it's just the fact that everyone you see is either depressed, dying, in pain or in labour. You rarely see a happy face and if you do it's because you've just seen somebody who's a biscuit short of a packet.

I followed the signs aimlessly to A & E and luckily found a helpful nurse who found me somewhere to wait. And wait I did, for bloody ages. I think they forgot about me.

I couldn't quite believe it when I felt a shadow hover over me and looked up to see Ollie standing there, bag in his hand.

"'Ello 'sis."

"Ollie, how did you know?"

"Debs called me. She thought I'd want to know, I've only been staying half an hour away." He gestured to the seat next to me. "Do you mind if I sit next to you?"

I shook my head.

"Where is the silly old sod then?"

"He's probably stuck on a trolley somewhere," I replied. "He's probably all by himself in a dark corridor wondering where the hell we are!"

"He's probably sleeping off the booze. He might not even know where he is."

"What if he's not? What if he has a blood clot in his brain or something that suddenly explodes and makes his heart stop?"

Ollie sighed. "You've been watching too much Casualty. He'll be fine, he just banged his head. They'll stitch him up and send him home."

"He's an old man. He could get complications"

Ollie turned to me and did something he's never done before: he took my hand. "He's not that old, Maz. And he's stronger than you think. He's not this fragile, little man. The fact is he drinks too much and is always doing daft things. He plays up this 'frail, old man' role."

"Yes, I know he drinks too much. Don't you think I know all about that?" I shot back. "It doesn't mean he hasn't got problems. He couldn't work when his back started to play up. But then you wouldn't know about that."

"I'm just saying…"

"But what are you just saying? Are you 'just saying' blame the booze. Dad is a drunk and that explains everything? You can't label people Ollie. You haven't even been here."

Ollie took his hand away. I could see his cheeks getting redder. "But you have to admit he drinks too much. He always did, even when I was there."

"Of course I admit that he drinks too much. What I'm saying is you shouldn't just label him as just another drinker. Nearly everything in life has let him down, his job, not being able to get another one, his back, Mum running off. You running off..." I stopped myself. "I'm sorry Ollie but he was so upset when you left home the first time, he drank even more. And it was me left picking up the pieces."

Ollie was quiet for a bit and then he said. "I didn't know that. I'm sorry."

"Well maybe it's time you should. You just disappeared one night, decided you were off to the city and that was it. And it would have been fine, but you never called. You never popped round for a visit. People would ask Dad how you were and he'd just shrug and say 'fine.' He knew you hated being with us, in our shabby, little house, with him a 'shabby, little man'. He told me once that he knew you were embarrassed by him."

"I was never!" Ollie jumped up, stood in front of me. "Don't you ever say that, because it wasn't true. He shouldn't have thought that."

"Well, why else did you move a few miles away and never even stay in touch."

"It just became easier that way." Ollie started pacing a short distance between our seats. "There are things you don't know, things just got a bit mad and it became easier to keep them separate from my home life."

Ollie sat down and took my hand again. "I hated living at home, it's true. I hated Dad drinking all the time when I was younger, although funnily enough it bothers me less now. I was a young lad and we clashed, things you probably didn't see. I blamed him for treating Mum badly. I could see she was unhappy, years before she left. When I was younger I just wanted to be rich and successful and I didn't want to be held back by a drunk, lazy Dad." He paused and rubbed my hand. "But that didn't mean I didn't love you all. I was just crap at talking and too bloody selfish for my own good. I just wanted to do my own thing and left you guys to get on with it."

By now I could feel tears running down my face, but didn't want to take my hand away to wipe them.

"I'm so sorry, Maisy," he said and I could hear his voice choking up too. "I've screwed up so much and all I want to do is try and make it better. I'm just not very good at it."

"Thank you," I whispered.

"There were so many things keeping me in London, a different life and I guess…"

"Miss Malone?"

A nurse had appeared before us, looking quite stern and scary. She was looking down at Ollie with a slightly scornful expression.

"I have your father here," she said, not bothering to wait for an answer. "I'm sure you want to see him. We need to run a few tests to be sure, but I think he will be fine."

I started crying again then. "Thank you nurse," I managed to splutter through the snot and fluid.

"I think maybe he should be more careful when drinking…" she stated, in a slightly haughty tone. "I think a lesson can be learnt."

As she walked away, Ollie wiped my tears away with the sleeve of his jacket.

"Don't mind her," he said. "If she laughed it would probably crack her face."

We walked into see Dad holding hands, before we entered the room Ollie kissed my cheek.

"When Dad is a bit better, we'll talk," he said. "And hopefully you'll understand."


**Comments**

**Popsicle:** I'm so glad your Dad is better

**007:** He had us all worried for a minute – see last blog


**Monday 21st November 2011**

**Daddy Day Care**

I have been forced to take some emergency leave from Pound4Pound so that I can make sure Dad is OK. According to the nurse, we have to make sure he doesn't show signs of concussion (sickness, feeling faint, confusion – the latter will be hard to determine). Luckily Dan was fine about it, he said that the shop was pretty quiet at the moment anyway, but they were keen to get me trained up before the Christmas rush. I'm not sure how much training shelf-stacking requires, but maybe I'm just being cynical.

Dad has been lying on the sofa in his favourite pair of Y-fronts, occasionally moaning in a dramatic fashion and insisting that he is kept refreshed with warm, sweet tea and seedless grapes.

"I'm a victim," he keeps saying. "The bloody council have not been maintaining their walls, one loose brick and over I went. Is that what I pay my taxes for? Broken walls? I could have been an elderly woman, with a dodgy hip – like Doris!"

"But why would Doris be walking on a wall?"

"That's not the point. If she *wants* to walk on a wall, she should be able to."

I have to admit the thought of Doris attempting to walk across a wall was quite an alarming one, knowing her she'd probably drag her bloody shopping trolley behind her. That thing seems permanently glued to her.

Just when I thought I might actually kill my own father (is death by suffocation possible with grapes?) and was cursing Ollie for doing one of his 'oh, I have somewhere I must be' speeches – the door flew open and in walked Debs from the Pride.

At first, I was shocked that she used the side door, even Nanna doesn't do that. I was also surprised at her dress. She is so short anyway, wearing such a low-cut/high cut (i.e. wafting the bottom cut) dress made it almost appear as if she wasn't wearing anything at all. Although I have to admit, for her age, she does have a good pair of legs. Better than mine in fact. (But that doesn't take much!) Her dark hair was piled high on her head and she had plastered on the make-up.

Dad shot up off the sofa and was obviously cursing the fact that he was languishing in his Y-fronts. He quickly grabbed the first thing to hand (which happened to be my pink and rather fluffy dressing gown) and threw it on.

"Debs," he gasped. "Delightful Debs. You came!"

"I brought you these," Debs replied, holding out more grapes and a copy of Viz. She obviously knows the man well, then.

I wonder why grapes are always offered to poorly people? They are hardly the safest of fruit. I've watched a pensioner nearly choke to death on one – mind you, he didn't have his teeth in, so he was trying to suck it too death. Surely an orange would be a safer option? Or a nice slice of melon?

Dad seemed happy though. He took the grapes and gave Debs a big hug. I noticed that his hands lingered around her bottom area. He kept gushing about how wonderful she looked.

"You don't look so bad either, Clive," she teased.

I was starting to feel a bit awkward.

One awkward moment was quickly replaced by another when the side door flew open (nearly knocking poor Dave off his feet) and Mum marched in. Mum was also dressed to kill in the tightest jeans I've ever seen her wear. But then again, when does my Mum ever dress down? She wears full make-up in bed.

"So where is the silly sod then, I…"

She strode into the room clasping her offering (a six-pack) and froze when she saw Debs and my Dad standing interlocked in the middle of the room.

"I'm sorry," she said in her super-polite voice. "I'll just drop this off and I'll go again."

"Don't be daft, Babs," Dad replied, adjusting the dressing gown over his grey and wrinkled chest. "Stay for a bit. Maz'll put the kettle on."

Oh yes, awkward just got worse.

I never thought my Mum would be bothered if Dad was to show interest in another woman. He had a brief fling with a woman from the laundrette, Eileen Springer, but she was an odd looking thing with a twitchy nose. I think Mum found that more amusing than threatening. Besides, that liaison only lasted a week.

No, there was something about Debs that was getting under Mum's nose. I could tell by the little sneering smile she had on her face.

"Are you enjoying running the pub?" Mum asked, still in her too-sugary tone.

"Loving it," replied Debs, beaming. "The locals are great fun. I'm hoping I can do loads for them. Get together some cabaret acts, maybe some bands."

"I'm in a band, I'm the singer." Mum shot back (I wanted to slap her if I'm honest).

"Really? Maybe you could do a slot for us. What are you called?"

"Blonde Streaks – we cover Blondie songs, amongst other Eighties' stuff. We're good." (No Mum, you're not.)

"Oh, OK....Well, I'll let you know. I'm guessing Clive has your details?"

"Well, of course he does. We were married for over twenty years" Mum said ever so sweetly, flashing a very false grin at my Dad.

"Yeah, until you buggered off with that bloke on the bike."

"OK, Clive..." Mum looked harassed.

"What was his name again?" Dad asked her.

"I don't...."

"I can't remember myself to be honest. I just know he had a shocking large nose. You could see his hooter coming round the street corner ten minutes before the rest of him. Didn't you used to hang your dirty knickers to dry on it?"

"Clive," Mum said sweetly. "There is no need to go down this road again, we have moved on now, haven't we."

"We sure have."

Debs smiled at my Mum. "I think it's nice that the two of you can get along so well. Me and my ex couldn't look at each other without shouting abuse at one another."

"Really?" Mum said, looking quite shocked. "That must be quite hard?"

"Not now, sweetie, he's dead." Debs seemed quite pleased. "The world is an altogether nicer place."

There was a bit of silence then, everyone sipped their teas (apart from Dad who was still munching his grapes noisily). Finally, my Mum decided to break the spell.

"I should tell you all while I'm here that we have set a date for the wedding. December the seventeenth. There is so much to sort out, but we wanted it to be as soon as possible." She giggled. "I'm crapping myself a bit, actually."

"Congratulations," said Dad, with a mouthful of grapes.

"I would love for you to come, Clive, and of course to bring a guest..." She flapped a hand loosely at Debs. The look she shot her, I reckon she's hoping Debs will be old news by then.

"And Maz, you have to come wedding dress shopping with me on Saturday. Tell that lump of a brother that he has to come too!"

And after a few hurried goodbyes, she was off. (I noticed she took the six-pack with her.)


## Comments

**007:** Oh dear, think your mum's nose was put out of joint. Good to hear your Dad is on the mend though.

**MaisyM:** Yes, he's back to his old self. Which is great (of course) but he is being annoying again now....


## Wednesday 23rd November 2011

### Nanna's Burning!

Work today was pretty good. Kept myself busy keeping the Christmas shelves restocked, it's amazing how many baubles and singing Santa's we have sold already. I liked being busy, it took my mind off Ollie and Dad and Jess and all the other rubbish going on at the moment.

Also, everyone here is so friendly, I feel like part of the team already. I am still about suspicious of Ruby though. She sneaks around the store checking up on everybody, but not doing an awful lot herself. Leon still seems scared of her and scampers away every time she comes near.

I've decided that Ruby must have some hold over Leon. She must know a secret or something. She certainly isn't a hard worker herself, she either walks up and down the aisles glaring at the customers (and basically scaring them), or she sits in the staff room sucking her fruit.

It's all a bit weird.

After work, I ran a hot bath because I was aching all over. I was planning a long soak (it might be my last one if these water meters are put in) but then I received a phone call from Nanna. To say she sounded upset would be like saying Dad sounded a little bit merry.

"It's been one of those days, Maisy," she complained.

"Oh Nanna – you've not been arguing with the neighbours again, have you?"

"No darling, although I'm still suspicious of that sneaky pair, I can tell you. I'm sure *she's* having an affair and as for the bloke? Well, he's just a weirdo."

"Nanna…"

"No, I'm not ringing about them. I'm ringing because I set fire to the bloody dining room."

"You what?" I was sure that I must have heard this wrong. "You did what?"

"I set light to the dining room." Nanna sounded rattled, understandably. "But it's not my fault. It's your Grandad's."

"How is it Grandad's fault? He's dead?"

"I know he's dead, what do you think I am; senile?" (I am beginning to wonder.) "It's his fault because he kept secrets from me, squirreled things away like the shifty bastard he was. And I would have never known if I hadn't attempted to light the fire in the dining room…"

"What, the smelly fire?"

We call it the 'smelly fire', because it's a big, old dusty fireplace that has never been used as far as I'm aware. Nanna used to say that Granddad banned them from using it, because it was too big and too expensive to run.

"Yes, that one. I was clearing out the room and was bloody cold in the room so I thought 'sod the silly bugger' and decided to light the fire. After 15 minutes, the room was full of smoke. What I didn't know was that the mean old git had stuffed loads of rubbish up the chimney. It all set alight, of course…"

"Crap? What like? Paper?"

"A bit like paper I suppose." Nanna took a breath. "No Maz, it was money. Lots of money."

I couldn't speak for a second. All I could think of was that this chimney had been rammed full of cash and we never knew.

"How much?" I whispered.

"I'm not sure," Nanna replied glumly. "Most of it was burnt to a cinder, but they reckon about a grand's worth."

"Oh, God…." I hissed. "Why didn't he tell you?"

169

"Who knows? Perhaps he thought he'd outlive me? Maybe he was planning to run off with it all one day, the greedy, no-good little…"

"Oh Nanna." I felt a little bit sick.

"It's not all bad. The firemen came quickly in their lovely uniforms and they were ever so helpful. They managed to get some of it back."

"Really?"

"Yes, really. I have some here that I can give Babs to put behind the bar for the wedding and a couple of hundred to help you out – I know it's not much but…"

"Nanna, it's wonderful. Thank you."

"Don't be daft. But you just wait until I see that git up in heaven, he'll regret the day he ever hid that cash from me!"

I don't for one minute doubt it.

After putting down the call from Nanna, I had another call from Dan.

"You OK?" he said. "You sound a bit glum."

"You know the expression, you lose a fiver but find a pound?"

"Er? No..."

"Oh, well. It kind of happened to me today."

"Aw, ok." Dan sounded very confused. "So this interview, it's on Monday, after work. That OK for you?"

"Er, yes. I guess so."

"If you like I can take you for a drink on Friday," he suggested casually. "Give you some tips. I'm not doing anything else."

"Erm. OK, if you're sure."

"Of course. I'd like to be able to help you, and it'll be hard to do it in the office."

"Cool. Friday will be fine then…"

To be honest I would have agreed to anything right then as I was feeling so fed up.

Maybe my luck is changing?

**Comments**

**Popsicle:** A date with the agent? OOO Maisy, you kept that one quiet.

**MaisyM:** It's not a date, he's just giving me some advice.

**007:** Lucky guy.

Sorry to hear about the money btw

**MaisyM:** That's ok – at least we got some of it back. I'm over it now, I think!

**Glen@LondonRiotCleanup:** Aw, I'm jealous. You're dating some agency guy. I still want to make you my cyber warrior.

**MaisyM:** It's not a date!!


**Friday 25th November 2011**

**My Date with Dan**

It was odd really, thinking about going for a drink with Dan. I know that we are good mates now and that he has helped me a lot with the jobs and everything, but even so, it's weird to suddenly be out socially with that person. I'm only used to talking to him at the end of the phone, or behind his messy desk.

I've never even seen his legs. For all I know he might not have any. Or they might be really short and stumpy. Or weirdly bendy.

We had arranged to meet in the centre of town by his offices. I was quite relieved to find that his legs were perfectly formed, as he walked towards me in his casual manner. His hair was as mad and scruffy as usual, but he looked nice in his dark jeans and black jacket.

"Hi," he said. "I'm glad you could come. I'm hoping that tonight I can help you get this job."

"You're certainly going to a lot of effort," I replied. "Do you do this with all your temps?"

"Only the ones I like," he smiled. "Look, I wanted to get out tonight anyway and I thought it would be a nice opportunity to have a chat and run past the job with you. Everything becomes easier over a drink."

"My Dad would certainly agree with you on that one."

We walked over to the nearest bar where Dan, as promised, ordered himself a beer and me an orange juice. I felt quite silly and young then.

"So this Neil fella," I asked. "What's he like?"

"OK in the main," Dan replied. "He's loaded and always bragging about his fast cars and his big house. But his heart is in the right place, I think."

"When you meet him on Monday, he's bound to run some role playing exercises past you. It's all common sense. You have to make sure that you come across as determined and money motivated."

"That makes me sound attractive," I moaned.

"It's just a game. You have to sell yourself. Convince him that you are confident, sassy and worth employing."

Dan ordered more drinks and thrust more advice my way. I was starting to feel a bit overwhelmed.

"You'll be fine," he told me, squeezing my hand. "I just have this feeling."

"You're psychic, are you?" I teased him.

"Oh yes, didn't you know?" He threw his head back in an elaborate fashion. "I have powers that the likes of you would never understand. And I can see great things for you, sitting on that little desk next to mine."

I smiled at him. "You've been a great help to me. Without you I'd still be at the job centre, convincing them that I would take anything."

"Aw, don't, you're making me blush." He took a swig of his beer. "To be honest I was doing crap until you came along. I hadn't made a placement in weeks and then you came and changed my luck."

"So, I guess we were lucky for each other then."

"Indeed. Cheers to that!"

We clinked glasses in a cheesy fashion and burst out laughing.

"Anyway," I said, deciding to move the conversation on a little. "Have you decided when you are moving in with Sadie?"

"Err…yes and no," he answered slowly. "Yes, I've made my mind up. No, I won't be moving in with her."

"Oh." I was surprised, although I was trying not to act it. "I take it she won't like that very much?"

"I'm guessing she'll hate me for it, but the fact is I'm just not ready. What's the point of doing something that your heart's not into? I'd only be lying to myself."

"But you love her, don't you, so…"

"I guess…I mean, yes, of course I do." He didn't sound convinced. "It's just so complicated. She's a beautiful girl and a lot of fun, but sometimes she's…well, so demanding. Every day is hard work. And it's not like we have a hell of a lot in common either…"

"Do you think it's because you don't work together anymore? Maybe you're drifting a little?" I suggested, concerned by his slightly pained expression. "It might just need some extra effort while you readjust. I mean, I don't know…I'm hardly a relationship expert."

He laughed. "You must be better than me."

"Don't bet on it. My last two 'experiences' have been with a man who's literally been suffocated by his mother's bosom and a boy from school who ended up dating the year psychopath."

Dan was laughing even more now. "You're right. It should be me giving you advice." He paused for a few minutes and then continued. "The thing is, you're right. We have been drifting. Sadie has such big ideas now that she is in the fashion world, I'm not really sure if I even fit in. But I do care for her. Why do things have to be so hard?"

"Because 'things' always are…"

"Ok." Dan leant forward, his eyes burning into mine. "So what about you, Maisy? You often talk about your family. How have they been lately?"

"God, the same as always. Brother has problems but I can't get hold of him to ask him about it, he's always out – although apparently he's going to talk to me soon. I have a Mum who is wedding obsessed. I don't see her now because she is constantly down the social club, making arrangements for the reception. And as for my Dad…"

"Well? Go on, I'm intrigued."

"Intrigued? He's the least intriguing person you'd ever meet. He's either watching crappy TV or he's down the local trying to impress the new landlady."

"You're family sound great," Dan said and then seeing my raised eyebrow, added "No, really!"

"You're welcome to them."

"You shouldn't say that. The grass is always greener. My parents are so dull I can barely find a word to describe them. Sometimes I think they are unaware of their own existence, let alone mine."

I smiled at him and he squeezed my hand. It's funny, how his dull family sounded delightful, they sounded normal.

It was getting late so Dan led me out of the pub, into the freezing cold night. I guess it was pure instinct that made him pull me nearer to him, so I didn't feel the chill of the wind.

He tipped up my chin ever so delicately, so that I was back looking directly into those clear, blue eyes of his. I could feel my tummy flip, which I wasn't expecting and we seemed to be frozen in that moment for ages.

"There's something about you, Maisy, I just can't..."

And that's when he bent down towards me. And it happened. It shouldn't have happened but it did, his lips delicately touched mine and just for a moment everything was perfect.

Except then his stupid, bloody phone went off. Really loud too, a blaring tune that dissolved the spark between us. Dan became flustered and looked at the screen. He's face went red.

"It's Sadie," he told me, almost apologetically. But he didn't answer the phone.

It didn't matter anyway. I knew then that that magical moment had gone.

"I'm off then!" I said brightly, pulling my coat tightly against me. "I can grab a tram from here."

I touched his arm gently and thanked him for a great night.

"Good luck on Monday," he replied softly. "I hope tonight helped."

I'm not sure whether I can answer that, because as I made my way home I felt more confused than ever. I couldn't stop thinking about the 'near-kiss' and the certain amount of attraction between us. But at the same time, I knew the reality was that

Dan was a good mate, in a long-term relationship, who could (maybe) become a work colleague one day.

Perhaps it is best that things are left, just the way they are.

## Comments

**Popsicle:** Aw, it's sooooo romantic. Like something from a film!!

**Glen @LondonRiotCleanup:** He sounds like a knob. He has a girlfriend after all. Don't waste your breath

**007:** I think he likes you. You don't know what's going on with his girlfriend. Maybe you should just ask him. He's a lucky fella.

**MaisyM:** Thank you but maybe I'm best off without further complications!

## Sunday 27th November 2011

### Just thinking...

You know what, the more I think about it, the more relieved I am that nothing more happened between me and Dan last night. I mean, how bloody awkward would had that been?

Anyway, on further reflection I have decided that his hair is far too scruffy. It would irritate me.

And he has very small hands. Should a man have small hands? Shouldn't they be big, hairy and...well...manly?

It's good that nothing happened. It's a really good thing.

I'm a happy person. Honest, I am.

I should just forget about him. Plenty more fish in the sea and all that.

What about my lovely followers. 007? The fat man in the kebab shop? Or the man of my dreams?

Who knows?...

## Comments

**Lucy Locket:** Aw bless. Think you are convincing yourself.

How is your mate Jess btw

**MaisyM:** She is fine. Doesn't want to go out much as she's feeling so sick, but her and Steve are spending loads of time together to try and work things out.

**007:** Ha ha – I could be your Prince Charming!

**MaisyM:** I hated Cinderella when I was a kid, preferred Beauty and the Beast!

**007:** Well, I can easily be the Beast! That's not a hard look to pull off!


### Wednesday 30ᵗʰ November 2011

### Interview with a Vampire

I went to work today, with my only suit neatly packed into a Sainsbury's bag. Hardly glamorous.

Jed was sat in the staff room, reading the 'situations vacant' in the local newspaper. He had his feet on the table and his usual sly look on his face.

"You looking for a new job then?" I asked, surprised. I thought Jed had been there for years. He seemed to blend in with the stockroom somehow.

"I'm always looking sweetheart, not that there's much bleedin' point. All the jobs here are for carers or bloody cleaners…Bad times."

"Tell me about it."

Jed looked me up and down then returned back to his newspaper with a disgruntled grunt.

"Seriously though, I spend my life looking at job vacancies. I swear half of those don't exist, they seem to just a re-hash of the same ads," I insisted.

"I guess we should be thankful we have something then, even if it is in this hole."

Jed then threw the paper and got up, simultaneously yawning and stretching his body in a rather exaggerated fashion.

I don't think anything really bothers Jed. He just lives on the day to day. Doing his job, putting a bet on a few times a week and having a pint with the lads.

Work itself seemed to drag as I was getting more and more nervous about my approaching interview. I tried to distract myself tidying tinsel and by trying to strike up conversation with Ruby, who was lingering behind me like a bad smell.

"Do you like Christmas?" I asked her, as I tried to restack several (quite broken) boxes of baubles.

"No, I hate everything about it," she sniffed and continued to stare at me.

"Oh. Do you not spend it with your family then?"

"No. I hate them too."

And with that she stalked off, probably looking to stalk Leon again. She's definitely an odd one. She's the sort I read about in my Mum's magazines. They hate the world and then end up murdering somebody in a horrific and bloodthirsty way.

By the time half five arrived, I was pretty hot and sweaty, having had to clean an aisle that had had milk spilt all down it, and then had to chase after a deranged three year old that had decided to run away from her heavily pregnant mum. I had to change into my crumpled suit in the staff toilets and stuff my sweaty clothes back into the Sainsbury's bag, which I left under the table in the staff room (I don't think carrier bags are a good look when you are trying to impress at interview).

By the time I got to Recruit4You, I felt pretty beaten already. I walked through the door and accepted the look of contempt that Snotty Sue flashed me. Her suit was beautifully pressed and delicately tailored. If I had been less of a woman, I would have stapled her pretty manicured hands to the desk and robbed her of it.

I looked around for Dan but he was nowhere to be seen. The office was in fact empty.

"We're closed now," Snotty said, by way of explanation. "Neil is seeing you after hours."

"Of course." *I knew that...*

I waited for a while feeling awkward and not even bothering to leaf through the glossy magazines this time. Finally, after about five minutes (but it felt like fifty) the door of the back office flew open and out strode the tallest man I have ever seen.

Not only is he tall, he is incredibly pale and very, very thin – waspish I think they call it. His hair is very, very dark liquorice and it looks like the texture of the sweet too. I almost wanted to lick it (but of course I didn't). And then he smiled at me and revealed his line of perfectly capped white teeth. Perfect, except for the fact that they were too big for his mouth.

I mean this might sound a bit far-fetched, but I swear he looks like a vampire. Not that I've met one lately or anything. But if I had, that's what they would look like. Poppy would have loved him; he looked like he had walked out the pages of her book.

I wish Dan had warned me, I would have dosed up on my garlic.

Neil led me into the back room with barely a word. My imagination was working overtime. We were alone, apart from Snotty Sue - and she doesn't count because she's not human either. What if he was to attack me? Could I defend myself with a biro and a packet of Tic-Tacs?

I think maybe I have been watching too many episodes of Twilight with Poppy.

"Thank you for coming," he finally said. Once we were sat in his rather drab office. "Dan has been telling me all about you."

"Really...oh, that's great."

"I think maybe it would be good for you to know a little about me..." He lent forward, his dark eyes widening. "I started with nothing you know. This company was made out of my back bedroom. I made contacts, developed a database. I *am* Recruit4You."

"That's...nice..."

"This is my passion, my energy, my drive. And I believe in it and everyone that works for it. If you work for me, I have to believe in you. Do you understand?"

"Yes, of course."

"So, selling is what it's all about in this industry." Neil suddenly produced a silver pen and handed it to me. "So, sell me this."

"Eh?"

"Sell me that pen."

"OK." I looked at the pen and felt a bit unnerved. "Would you like this pen? It's very nice?"

"No, thank you," he replied firmly.

"Oh." I sat back. That didn't seem very fair.

"Don't give up. Persuade me!"

"Go on. It's a nice pen. It's shiny."

"Tell me it's USP."

"It's what?"

"Unique selling point!" I think he was getting frustrated.

I looked at the pen again. I've never sold pens before. This was a recruitment job.

"Err…It looks better in your hand than this piece of tat…" I threw my battered and chewed Bic onto the desk. We both looked at it for a second.

I can't remember much else. I answered the rest of the questions politely and as quickly as I could. I just wanted the interview to be over. Neil didn't smile at me again.

I think we can say that I truly screwed that one up.

And I still have his bloody pen.


**Comments**

**Popsicle:** I WANT TO MEET NEIL

Can I have an interview please??

**Lucy Locket:** It might not have been as bad as you thought…

**007:** I bet you did better than you thought. Fingers crossed.


**Friday 2nd December 2011**

**No News is Bad News**

I have had no call from Dan, so I am assuming my instinct was right. I messed up that interview. I guess the world of sales was never going to be for somebody like me. I'm a bit frustrated though, as it would have been nice to have had some feedback one way or another.

Luckily Leon told me today that they would probably need me up until Christmas, which is good. I have been putting little bits away to buy presents, and knowing I should get another few weeks' work is reassuring.

So far my Christmas list is looking pretty mean, but I really haven't got much to spend. I'm hoping that I can get the majority of it on Ebay. These are the ideas so far:

**Dad – Beer**

**Mum – Breakfast at Tiffany's on DVD**

**Sweaty Keith – More smellies....**

**Nanna – Subscription to Private Eye**

**Poppy – A love songs CD**

**Jess – Perfume**

**Dave – A couple of pigs ears (yuck)**

The only person I'm stuck on is Ollie. What do I get him? Even though he's back, he's hardly been here. He is like a fleeting shadow in our lives. I think he only pops in and out to prove that he's not disappearing again.

I also have the worry of Mum's wedding present. She rang in a panic today, moaning about the stuff she still had to sort out, and checking I was able to come to her hen night next weekend. Luckily I can bring the girls with me. I think a night with Mum's mates down at the Indian might just finish me off.

"I just want everything to go alright; tell me it will be okay, Maisy," she pleaded down the phone to me.

Of course I said it would it be. I told her that it would be fab and that she had nothing to worry about. All the time I was looking at the sofa where Ollie had been laid out a few weeks ago, knowing that I still had to talk to him.

Why were we both putting it off?

*Comments*

**007:** Just grab the bull by the horns and talk to him.

BTW – no news is good news!

**Monday 5ᵗʰ December 2011**

**Still Waiting…**

No word from Dan. I'm beginning to think he might be avoiding me. Maybe he is embarrassed after our drinks last Friday? Or maybe my interview went so badly that he is irritated with me. Neil may have had a go at him for recommending me in the first place. He could be really annoyed.

I could call him, but I can't.

I don't know why this is bothering me so much. It shouldn't be.

Please call soon…

*Comments*

**Lucy Locket:** Aw babe – you'll hear soon

**007:** Stop worrying, there's bound to be a reason and talk to your brother instead!

**Tuesday 6ᵗʰ December 2011**

**Ollie**

I can honestly say that the last person I expected to find waiting outside work for me today was Ollie. He was just sitting there, on the small wall that runs alongside the shop, his rucksack nestled between his legs.

His head was bent down slightly so I almost walked past him and only noticed he was there at the last second.

"Ollie?"

He lifted his head slowly and I was shocked at just how tired and grey he looked. He appeared to have lost weight from his face. His cheeks looked like they were actually sinking into themselves and his eyes had dark smudges under them.

My first thought was 'oh no, he's ill.' But I couldn't ask. To be honest, I wasn't sure if I wanted to know.

He stood up and walked over to me, slowly.

"Come on, let's take a walk. It's time we talked."

We ended up walking through the local park. Ollie didn't want to 'sit inside anywhere.' He said he felt too restless. For a while we didn't talk, we just walked beside one another.

For that time of the day the park was pretty busy, with plenty of children still playing in the large fields and many others, like us, taking leisurely walks up the various paths. I love late autumn – the crisp, cold feel of the air, the beautiful colours, the smells, the promise of even colder weather to come.

"God, I need some sunshine," Ollie grumbled, as if reading my mind.

"Aw, I love this weather. It's so fresh and clean."

"Nah, it's bleak and depressing. I should be a bear and just hibernate for the coldest months, my body hates it. I want to be somewhere hot. Last year I was in Mexico over Christmas, surely you'd prefer that?"

I shrugged.

"I love Mexico. And Thailand. Actually, I think I preferred Thailand, there was so much to see. Such beautiful beaches."

"The furthest I've been is Southend," I told him.

Ollie stared at me for a bit and then said, "I'm sorry Maz, I wasn't thinking. I didn't mean to sound boastful."

"It's OK."

He led me to a bench in a small shaded area, next to a pretty purple bush. There was a small plague on the bench that read 'Henry Noble – he loved sitting here.'

"Dad would have one of those on his bar stool," I said, feeling a bit sad.

"Or his bloody armchair," Ollie replied. "If it doesn't collapse by then."

We laughed and it was nice. I was glad to have him back. I realised then that I had not called him 'the arsehole' for ages. I think I know now just how much I missed him.

"I have something to tell you." Ollie said. "It's something I should have said a long time ago, but I just kept putting it off…and now…well, it's getting harder to say…"

"What? What is it?"

He was looking at his hands now, not at me. My stomach was churning, wondering if I would be able to take whatever he was going to throw at me.

"I'm gay."

"Oh….oh…Ollie, for God's sake!"

I couldn't help it, the words just tumbled out. Ollie looked at me with shock.

"I'm sorry, Ollie, but Jesus…" I drew breath. "I thought you were going to tell me you were dying or something."

"So you're OK about it?"

"Yes, of course. Why wouldn't I be? I mean…I'm surprised. Why did you make such a big thing about it? Why didn't you tell me earlier?"

"I'm not sure. I haven't admitted it to myself for long, and it's been so easy just to carry on."

"And Lottie?"

Ollie sighed. "I was with Lottie and I did really care for her, but not in the way I should have done. I did an awful thing to her. She'll never forgive me…"

"Oh no. What?"

"I had a fling with her brother, Ben."

"Oh no… and she found out?"

"Yeah, she caught us in bed together." Ollie looked away, obviously embarrassed.

"Bloody hell. No wonder she kicked you out," I muttered.

"And that's what I've been trying to sort out. I've wrecked a family. Me and Ben, we liked being with each other but I hate what we've done to Lottie. I'm hoping one day she'll understand."

"So you went back to London to work it out with him?"

Ollie nodded. "But I'm not sure…we might have to give it some time. It's so complicated."

"But what about Jess?"

"Jess wasn't a girlfriend. We would just go out and talk. We get on so well, I think of her like...Oh I don't know..."

"A sister?" I was surprised how hurt I felt when I said that.

"Maybe. You were so closed to me and I just wanted someone I could be myself with, Jess was that person. I never told her I was gay, but I think she guessed."

"Jess is one of the smartest people I know," I said to him, taking his hand in mine. "I'm glad you finally told me."

"Me too. The only thing is, I want to tell everyone else now. I'm not so worried about Mum and Nanna, but what about Dad?"

I thought about this. "Dad is...well, Dad. He will take it his own way. But I'm sure it will be fine."

Ollie then leant forward and kissed the top of my head.

"After all the crap you've been put through, you've been fantastic, Maz. I'm going to make it up to you, I promise."

And do you know what. I really do feel, for the first time in my life, that I have got a brother.

**Comments**

**007:** Finally, you've talked. Don't you feel better now?

**MaisyM:** Yes and guilty and sad. I wish we'd done it a long time ago now.

**Wednesday 7th December 2011**

**Gay Pride**

Ollie decided that there was no time like the present. He wanted the family to know. He was sick of hiding his sexuality like it was a nasty perversion.

"I want you there with me though, Maz," he insisted. "I can't bottle out of this. I want to go to the wedding as 'me'."

It was lucky that today was my day off.

We figured that we would visit Nanna on the way to Mum's. It's usually best to catch her in the mornings, as she tends to go to her Neighbourhood Watch Meetings in the afternoons.

"They're a group of nosey bastards," she told me. "But I get a nice slice of cake from Maureen Dempsey and I get a legitimate excuse to keep an eye on those dodgy neighbours of mine."

Not only is Nanna convinced that one of them is having an affair, she now suspects that they are tax fiddlers to boot.

When we arrived, I could tell Ollie was nervous because he was picking at the skin round his nails. He's not seen Nanna at all since he's been back, knowing that she disapproved of his vanishing act. Nanna was watching some political programme when we walked in, shouting abuse at some red-faced MP.

"These monkeys don't know they're arses from their....oh, look what the cat's just brought in..." She eyed Ollie somewhat suspiciously. "I was wondering when you was going to show your face."

"Hello, Nanna," Ollie replied politely and sat down next to her.

I busied myself making us all tea, leaving them both to talk. I could hear snippets of the conversation. I could hear Nanna telling him off for 'becoming one of the prats in the city' and 'forgetting his own family.' I also heard muttered apologies from Ollie and admittances that he had indeed 'been a prat, for quite some time.'

When I re-entered the room, mugs in hand, Ollie looked up at me and then back at Nanna again (who was by now engrossed in her programme again).

"Nanna, I wanted to tell you that I'm gay," he said, in quite a matter-of-fact manner.

"You're what?" Nanna was still watching the screen, obviously distracted by an argument that was developing on the panel. "This bloody idiot doesn't have a leg to stand on. He's jabbering on about education reforms, yet he's been privately educated all his life. Bloody buffoon."

"I'm gay, Nan."

"Are you?" Nanna looked over at him. "Hmm, would make sense I suppose, all that suppressed anger of yours. Pretty girlfriends, but not much coming from any of it. I should have guessed long ago."

"You don't mind?"

"Mind? Why should I mind?" She leaned forward and touched Ollie's hand. "Love is love. Just as long as you're happy I don't care what type of packaging it comes in. I just want you to be happy and stop sodding about."

"So do I," he replied softly.

"I thought about being a lesbian myself, once," Nanna continued. Seeing the look of horror on my face she smiled. "It did exist in my day too, you know. A beautiful woman called Geraldine Young once made it known to me that she would like to…well, you know... But, the trouble is, I've always been a meat and two veg type of woman, if you get my drift…"

Ollie burst out laughing. "Why was I ever worried about telling you?" he asked.

"Because like most men, you're an idiot," she said. "But I love you for it."

Telling Mum after that visit was so much easier, as Ollie was on a high. He just walked into Mum's flat, past Sweaty Keith on the sofa and straight over to Mum in the kitchen.

"Mum, I'm gay."

Mum, being Mum, shrieked like a demented bird.

"Oh, Ollie – are you really? I always wanted a gay son!"

I'm not sure if Ollie was completely chuffed with that reaction, but at least it was kind of positive.

"I always knew really," she told us, once she had composed herself. "You always preferred playing with my dresses and my bags than with cars."

"Eh? Are you one of those transsexuals then?" asked Sweaty Keith, obviously confused.

"No. I'm gay. It doesn't mean I like wearing dresses."

Sweaty Keith nodded, obviously relieved at this answer.

"Oh, Ollie. We can go shopping together. We can go to Gay Pride marches. Will you take me to that Heaven Club? I've always wanted to go there?" Mum was rambling and getting more and more excited. Ollie meanwhile, was looking paler by the second.

"This is such wonderful news. If only I had known sooner, I could have got you a special pink suit for the wedding. I've seen Elton John in one similar."

We left Mum's soon after dinner. Actually I think it was shortly after Mum suggested that Ollie lead the YMCA dance at the reception.

"She's stuck in the Eighties," I said by way of explanation.

"She's stuck somewhere, I'm not sure it's anywhere in reality," Ollie moaned.

He was hoping to score the hat trick and tell Dad as well, but as usual, Dad was down the Pride – a short note, blue-tacked on the fridge told us to expect him back late. This also meant he'd be drunk.

"It'll have to be tomorrow now," Ollie decided. "But he's the one I dread telling the most."

Considering Dad still refers to gay men as being 'bent as a nine bob note,' Ollie's not the only one dreading tomorrow's 'outing.'


## Comments

**Lucy Locket:** Good luck telling your dad – I'm sure it'll go better than you think

**Popsicle:** Maybe you should buy him a few drinks first?

**007:** He might just surprise you. Make sure your Mum doesn't buy that Elton John suit or you'll never see Ollie again!


## Thursday 8th December 2011

### Father and Son

I was half hoping that Ollie would talk to Dad while I was at work today. Not because I didn't want to be supportive, because I do, of course I do. But I wondered if it would be easier for them to talk freely if I wasn't there.

Also, I had a rubbish day and I wasn't in the best of moods walking home. Jed was back to his lecherous old self again. Today, he brushed past me in the corridor and 'accidently' placed his hand on my boob again.

"Oh dear, what's that doing there?" he said, with a dirty grin.

"Take your hand off," I hissed back.

Jed immediately flung both of his arms up in the air in a defensive action. "Oh dear, look at Miss Sensitive. I only brushed past you. Are you too high and mighty to be touched now?"

I tried to tell Leon but he just went bright red, started to fiddle with his glasses and admitted 'he wasn't quite sure what he could do.'

*Oh I don't know Leon, perhaps you could discipline the nasty little weasel? Just a thought…*

I would tell Dan, but he still hasn't called. I really think I have scared him off.

So all of this put me in a foul mood and not really in the state of mind for a big family meeting. Therefore, I was sorely disappointed to come home and find Dad and Ollie sitting at home watching The Weakest Link. Ollie flashed me a look that said, *'Sorry, not done it yet.'*

I threw down my coat and flopped down in the seat next to him. I was so tired my bones hurt. There was no way I as making them tea as well.

"There's something quite sexy about that Anne Robinson," my Dad announced. "I think it's her menacing presence. She looks like she would give you a good time and then give you a good telling off for it."

"And that's a good thing?"

Dad sniggered. "Sometimes, love."

Ollie was shuffling uneasily beside me. I poked him in the ribs and then glared at him. Ollie glared back and mouthed *'wait'* at me. I sighed and sat back in my seat.

"These bloody questions are too simple, Dave could answer them," Dad was moaning.

Dave looked up at the mention of his name. He was lying under the table with his legs in the air, showing off the white of his belly. He wasn't exactly striking me as some kind of animal genius.

"Dad…" Ollie said finally.

"Mmmmm?"

"Dad. Don't you want to know why I went back to London?"

Dad flapped his hand at Ollie dismissively. "You told me. You had stuff to sort out. I don't need to know the ins and outs of your life…"

"Yes, but there are some things you need to know."

"Really, son, I don't." Dad was still looking at the T.V, but it was as if he was looking through it, not actually watching it anymore.

"I'm…"

"Gay? Yes, I already know."

Ollie looked stunned. "How? Did Mum tell you?"

Dad shook his head; his cheeks had turned bright red. "I heard you on the phone rowing one afternoon. It sounded like a lover's tiff and you got really upset. You threw the phone down and I couldn't help myself, I looked at it and saw the last caller was a fella. I might not be the brightest spark, but I worked it out."

"But?"

"But nothing. I guess part of me always knew. A parent always does."

Ollie was pacing the room now, running his hands through his hair. "I wish I'd told you earlier, now. If I'd known how well you'd have taken it…"

"So this Lottie bird, you're not telling me 'she's' a 'he' are you?" Dad looked confused.

"No, of course not."

"'Cause I'm not sure how I'd explain that one to the lads down the pub…" He paused, obviously mulling the thought over. "Not that I should give two hoots what they think. Norm's son likes nicking underwear off the washing lines…"

"So it could be worse," I said sweetly. Ollie flashed me a look that suggested this was not such a great comment to make.

At that moment, Dad stood up and took Ollie's hand, shaking it firmly.

"Really," Dad said softly. "I don't give a flying what-sit what you are, as look as you are happy and healthy. You're my son."

Ollie immediately hugged him. "Thank you Dad, that means everything."

"Oh, and don't go thinking that you can bugger off again like you did before," Dad said, with a wry smile.

I think both of them have reached a good place and have a better understanding of each other.

The only way is up now…

## Comments

**Lucy Locket:** Told you. So fab that they have worked this out

Meantime you need to sort out Jed, report him. What a creep!

**MaisyM:** You're right, he is a creep but I don't like causing trouble

**Lucy Locket:** Stop being so nice all the time

BTW I've got a job finally!! Admin job at the local council – so excited.

**MaisyM:** That's great news. Congratulations


## Friday 9th December 2011

### Meeting of Mates

Jess and Poppy popped in during my lunch break. We walked over to McDonalds and I treated Jess to a Big Mac (she has a craving for meat).

Once we'd sat down, I looked at both of them with a raised eyebrow.

"Yes," Jess said, understanding the gesture. "I have talked to Poppy and explained everything, not that I needed to as it's all documented in your blog anyway."

"Yes, Maisy has been keeping me updated in her own unique way but I have been slack lately and I'm sorry," Poppy said sorrowfully, all big eyed. "But it's so hard when you're a struggling author. You know I love you both."

"Oh, give over Pops! You'll start my morning sickness off again," Jess moaned, rubbing her tummy. "I've not exactly been around much anyway. I can barely face leaving the house."

"I'm not even pregnant, but I'm feeling queasy too," I added.

"Anyway, changing the subject from Miss Soppy Knickers, I've told Mum about the baby too," Jess said, now between mouthfuls. "She wasn't pleased."

"What did she say?" I asked

"That I was a silly cow that had screwed her life up and hadn't I listened to anything she'd told me." Jess took another bite, chewing loudly. "I think she thinks I've turned out like her. She had me at seventeen, didn't she."

"So? You're different."

"Exactly, and that's what I told her. Me and Steve are going to try and make it work. He's got an apprenticeship now at the garage and I've put my name down on the council waiting list."

"What about your job?"

"I'll work until I'm ready to push. I'm pregnant, not ill. I'm not feeling too bad at the moment. Once the baby comes I'm hoping to do my beauty course like I planned."

I have to admit, Jess is looking pretty good. Her face has a nice fresh look to it and she seems happy, relaxed.

I watched as Jess continued to devour her burger. I had only ordered fries. I wasn't that hungry and Big Macs always gave me heartburn for some reason. I didn't fancy burping the taste of onions all afternoon (although it might act as a deterrent to Jed – then again, knowing my luck he would find it attractive). Poppy was picking at her burger delicately, while glancing at her phone every ten seconds. She thought we wouldn't notice. But we did.

"I've spoken to Ollie," I said finally.

Jess wiped away the dribble of juice on her chin. "And what did he have to say for himself?"

"Well...he's... erm, come out."

Jess took this in for a second, looking confused. Then her mouth twitched and she burst out laughing.

"Jess!"

"Well, it's a relief to be honest. I was beginning to think I had lost my touch. Once, I touched him and he actually flinched. I've never had that effect on blokes before, it was worrying me."

"Well now you know."

"I told you something was wrong. I knew it wasn't just an ex-girlfriend winding him up."

I had to go back to work then, and Jess had shopping to get too. She wanted to look at baby stuff (even though she was too suspicious to get anything yet) and she needed more comfortable bras, as her boobs had already grown in size (lucky cow!). Poppy said she would help her. I was glad, as I think they need some time together.

We all had a big hug outside the shop and I breathed in the mixed smell of the grease, burger and perfume that lingered on them.

I love these girls so bloody much.


## Comments

**Popsicle:** We love you tooooo xxx

**JesseBelle:** Most of the time anyway

I can't believe this blog is still going....


## Saturday 10th December 2011

### Curried Hens

Tonight was Mum's hen's night. I'm writing this at one in the morning, feeling a little worse for wear. I apologise now if there are any spelling errors or typos. To be honest, the screen is moving a bit, but I can't face bed yet. I feel a bit sick and at least this is taking my mind off things.

It was a good night. Better than I thought it would be. And Mum enjoyed herself, despite being dressed as a complete tit, condoms on her head, learner plates – the works. She looked like Ann Summer's nightmare.

There was quite a group of us. Jess in her skin-tight trousers (enjoying it while she can), Poppy in an eye-catching red, low cut dress, Rene in a mini dress with her boobs swaying over the top – and Mum in a white fairy outfit. She looked like she'd lost her Christmas tree. Mum had also invited Nanna (who was the smartest, in a pale, pink trouser suit), Maureen, another club singer with hair so high she terrifies birds, Patty (who's married to Bob and only talks about Bob) and Cheryl, Mum's hairdresser – very loud but very funny.

We took over the Barji House, spreading over the long table like a drunken disease, necking Cobras like it was going out of fashion. We also ate the hottest and tastiest curries on the menu (apart from Poppy who can only stomach a Korma, due to her delicate stomach lining).

"This is this best night ever!" Mum announced, halfway through our meal. One condom from her custom-made hat was already draping over her right eye. "I have such wonderful friends. And family...I don't know what I would do without you!"

We all made the dutiful '*aw*' noise until Maureen interrupted.

"Enough of this soppy crap. We want to hear the dirt. What is it about Keith that rocks your boat?"

Everyone burst into laughter then, except me. I was cringing, thinking 'I really don't want to hear about my Mum and Sweaty Keith in that way, thanks all the same...'

"Ooo he's an ANIMAL!" my mother roared. "He presses all of my BUTTONS!"

A few other tables looked over at us, obviously concerned at what company they were keeping tonight. One grim-faced woman even shifted her chair slightly, as if terrified that our bawdiness was contagious.

"He's just like my Bob," said Patty, predictably. "I think it's because he's a water sign. He's so emotionally-tuned"

"Oh no, give me fire any day," argued Mum. "A fire sign has the passion and the desire. I can't be doing with romance and love letters."

"Do you know what," Mum said to us all, leaning forward to include us all in her revelation. "When I first met Keith, I thought he was a great lump of a man. All shiny and wide. I was with that idiot at the time, the one with the long nose... But he was more interested in gambling than in me. He loved those bloody horses. In fact, I think he would have liked me better if I had walked around the flat in a saddle and a harness."

"Oooo, kinky," said Maureen. "I once knew a man who liked something similar – but I drew the line when he wanted me to bleat."

Mum was laughing. "No, but seriously – Keith was one of his mates, always hanging around the flat, borrowing DVD's and stuff. We used to talk and we found out we both liked similar music. It's nice to have something in common. Then one evening while the idle so-and-so was down the betting shop, Keith asked me to move in with him. The rest, as they say, is history..."

"Aw, that's sweet," said Poppy. "You were obviously meant to be together."

"Maybe. But the best thing for me was that he supported me. He supported me performing in a band. Not only that, he believed in me. He's the only man who ever has."

The table fell silent for a bit then. That was until Maureen called the waiter over and threatened to show him her nipples unless he brought more poppadums over. The poor lad looked mortified.

We staggered out of there just after midnight, the last to leave. After serenading the staff with several songs including 'I've Had The Time of My Life' and 'Lady in Red.' We offered to take Mum to a club, but she had only drunk the best part of two bottles of wine and was beginning to look a little green. Rene took her and Nanna home instead. Nanna was also looking a bit wobbly and was attempting to chat up the rather stiff and disapproving owner of the establishment.

I got the bus back with Poppy and Jess. None of us felt like going on anywhere.

Once home, I checked to see if Dad was in (he was – on his bed fully clothed and snoring) and Ollie was laid out watching some horror film on TV.

"Good night?" he asked.

"Yeah," I said. "Surprisingly, it was."

Who'd have thought I'd have had such a laugh with my Mum?


### Comments

**Popsicle:** It was a great night. Your mum is fab

**Glen @LondonRiotCleanup:** I wish I was a girl and I could've come, sounded great. And I love a curry

**MaisyM:** It was a great night...

**007:** Sounds it. Your Mum is obviously happy now too.

**MaisyM:** Yeah, I guess she is...

## GRRRRRR!!

I called Recruit4You today. I decided that I had waited too long without hearing any feedback. Surely I deserved to hear something, even if it was that I was total rubbish?

I must say that my opinion of Dan has dropped significantly. All that crap about me 'being great for the job.' And now that it's clear that I haven't got the job. He obviously can't be bothered with me anymore. He has cast me aside like a dirty tea towel. Actually, that reminds me, I must pick up some packets of those tomorrow at work. The ones in the house are so gross; they are growing some kind of new species...

The call did not go well – mainly because Snotty Sue answered the phone.

"Hello, Maisy," she sighed. "I'm afraid Dan isn't in right now, can I help?"

"Erm, is Neil there then?"

"No. He's in Australia. He will be for the next few weeks now."

"Oh...OK. It's just, I had an interview there last week...I wondered....well, I was wondering if I could get some feedback?"

"Oh." I swear I could actually hear her grinning. "Well I'm afraid that won't be possible right now. Neil would have briefed Dan and Dan isn't in at the moment."

"Do you know when he will be?"

"No. But I will be sure to tell him that you called." Her voice was laced with sweetness.

I hate that woman.

Hate her, hate her, hate her.

That cow probably knows I didn't get the job and just wants to make me suffer.

Well, screw them.

I don't need them....

## Comments

**Lucy Locket:** It doesn't sound fair though. You should call back and demand feedback.

**Glen @LondonRiotCleanUP:** This agent guy is messing you around. You should complain. Probably his girlfriend found out he had the hots for you and now he's too scared to speak to you again...

**MaisyM:** Nah, surely not??


## Thursday 15ᵗʰ December 2011

## Bloody, Bloody Dan

I was on my way into work today when my phone rang. I couldn't quite believe it when I saw the number: Dan. I was tempted not to answer, thinking 'I don't want to hear about one of your new assignments. I don't need you anymore.'

But the reality is I do need him. This job is ending. The job market is in big trouble and I need money. Therefore I couldn't afford to give Dan the finger, even though I really wanted to right then.

"Maisy," he sounded breathless and croaky when I answered. "I'm so glad I've got through to you. I was worried it would be your voicemail."

"Well, here I am," I said brightly. Too brightly perhaps.

"Listen, I'm sorry about the last few weeks, but Sue explained didn't she?"

"Snot...er, I mean Sue said that you were out of the office, if that's what you mean?"

"No, not really. I asked her to..." There was a pause. "Hang on a sec, did Sue not call you to explain I was ill?"

*Ill? No, Snotty didn't say that. What a Cow-face...*

"No, she didn't."

"She didn't tell you I couldn't even speak?" Dan sounded furious.

*Now I was feeling really really bad.*

"No, Dan, I knew nothing. I just assumed I'd messed up and that you didn't want to tell me."

196

"Oh God, no. Maisy, I wouldn't do that." He sighed and then hissed. "I'm going to kill that stupid woman."

*Oh yes, please do....*

"The truth is. I've not heard from Neil. The thing is, I got ill with this throat infection, some complication of tonsillitis, so Neil and I never got to talk. Now he's flown out for a holiday in Australia."

"Oh," I wasn't sure what to say. "Are you okay now?"

"Yeah, dosed up on antibiotics, in hospital for a bit, but fine...Anyway, we need to sort you out. This is not a bad sign, Maisy. Neil was in no hurry to fill this role; he was probably waiting to speak to me, that's all."

"I'm sure I messed it up though. I answered everything wrong."

"Nah, I wouldn't worry. I burped in the middle of my interview with him. He's more laid back than he appears. Leave this with me and I'll get back to you as soon as I can."

"Really, you'd do that for me?"

"Of course. It's my job to get you a job, isn't it?"

I think I like Dan again.

Just a little bit.


*Comments*

**Glen @LondonRiotCleanUp:** Hmm, sounds like a big fat excuse to me...

**MaisyM:** He did sound really, really croaky....

**Lucy Locket:** I'm glad you've heard. Let's hope you get some feedback soon x


## Friday 16th December 2011

### Manic Mummy

On the way out to work this morning I saw a formal looking envelope waiting for Ollie on the mat. I left it on the table for him, but I'm worried. The letter has 'private and confidential' stamped all over it and looks very official. I hope he's not in trouble.

When I came home, the letter had gone and there was no sign of Ollie either. I have a bad feeling that something has happened.

I didn't have time to sit and wait for him to come back though, as Mum was expecting me round. She wanted me to spend her last evening as a single woman with her. I was quite chuffed, until I found out that she asked Rene first, but Rene had pulled out because she had an urgent bikini line crisis.

I still went, though. I didn't like to think of my Mum alone on the night before her wedding.

Mum ordered in pizza and flicked through the channels looking for some naff TV for us to watch. It made me think back to when I was a kid, when I used to snuggle up on her lap watching Disney movies.

"Mum, do you remember watching Aladdin?" I asked.

"Oh God, yes. What was that song we used to sing?"

*"A whole new world,"* we both sung together and laughed.

"I suppose that's what I'm entering now…a whole new world," Mum muttered sadly.

"You're only worrying. It's natural the night before the wedding. You're only marrying him, nothing will change."

"But that's just it. Sometimes when you put a ring on their finger, they do change. Look at your Dad."

"But you were happy once, I remember," I protested.

"Yeah…We had our good days, I guess. But mainly it was painful. We rowed so much. Clive is very…well…he's just Clive, isn't he! Everything about him just started to grate."

"So why did you stay with him so long then?" I asked angrily.

"Because he could be lovely at times and he made me laugh. He was always grumpy, but funny. In the early days it was easier; we'd go to the pub together and put the world to rights. It's different when you're left at home on your own with the baby and he's still down the pub."

"But you stayed?"

"I stayed until you were old enough not to need me anymore. It came to a point when I couldn't stay a moment longer."

I wanted to tell her that I 'always needed her' and that she left right at the time when having a Mum was vital. How could I talk to Dad about PMT or boyfriends or spots? But I saw the sad look on my Mum's face and I remembered that it was her 'special day tomorrow' and decided to keep my mouth firmly shut.

"So," asked Mum brightly, obviously keen to change the subject. "What about you, Maisy? Any men on the horizon?"

"Nah, I'm afraid not."

"Really? Not even a sniff?"

"Not really."

"Not really? So there could be?"

"Stop fishing Mum! There's no-one. I mean, there's a guy I thought was quite nice, but he has a girlfriend and seems pretty committed to her. Apart from that, they're all idiots!"

"Well, you have to kiss a lot of frogs – just look at me," Mum gushed.

Hmm, looks like she's just progressed onto a greasy toad rather than a prince though.

I didn't stay late, as Mum wanted to make sure she got her full night's sleep – or else she would have 'massive shopping bags' under her eyes. I was quite relieved though, as I was feeling pretty tired myself.

As I was going to the door, Mum rushed into the bedroom.

"Wait there, Maisy, I want to give you something."

I stood there like a lemon, listening while she turfed out half of her wardrobe, swearing as she did so. Finally she re-appeared, her hair standing weirdly on end and her eyes wild with jubilation.

"Here it is!" she said, holding aloft a smallish purple book. "I want you to have this. It's the diary I kept during my last year living with Clive. It might answer some of your questions."

I took the diary, almost in disbelief that she had given it to me. It felt like the Holy Grail.

She kissed me gently on the cheek.

"I hope one day you will understand what I did Maisy. Maybe you'll even get to understand me better. God help, someone has to."

I'm not sure when I will read it. In some ways, I'm almost too scared to.


## Comments

**Popsicle:** You have her diary? My god how exciting. Have you looked yet?

**MaisyM:** No, I don't think I'm ready yet. It's stuffed under my bed.

**JesseBelle:** Wait until you feel strong babe – you might not like all that you see x


## Saturday 17th December 2011

### Mum's Getting Married …

And so the wedding day has arrived. Well, actually to be precise it's been and gone, because I'm writing this on Sunday. I didn't have a chance to write all day, it was so hectic. I'm feeling pretty groggy now and I'm having to soak my feet in warm water as my toes were not designed to wear heels all day.

Yesterday was a day of many things. It was joyous at times, it was often cringeworthy – but was also surprising.

Me and Ollie were being taken to the town hall by Rene and her new fella, Lionel. Of course we had to leave a complaining Dad behind. He was trying to decide whether he 'could be arsed to come to the reception or not.' His concern was that he didn't want to see Babs 'lording it over him,' but at the same time, he was worried that if he didn't attend it might look as if he was 'sobbing into his beer.'

We left him actually ironing his best shirt and pants, so I knew then that he would be going. I was surprised he even knew where the iron lived, let alone how to work the thing.

Ollie was complaining all the way in the car about his top hat, saying that it was 'making his head itch like a bastard.' He was worried that the congregation would think he had nits. He did look smart though. Mum was right; there was something quite beautiful about a man with golden curls wearing a posh hat.

Mum arrived on time, which was a miracle in itself. She came with Nanna in a black cab and she looked bloody gorgeous, I felt really proud of her. For once she looked dignified and serene (apart from the shock of bright red lipstick). Nanna also looked lovely, dressed smartly in a navy dress and matching hat.

I wasn't so sure about Mum walking up the Registry Office aisle to 'Take My Breath Away,' especially as she insisted on singing along. I guess this is quite an apt choice considering the aroma that tends to waft from Sweaty Keith's body. He's certainly taken my breath away on more than one occasion. I was even less sure about Sweaty Keith's choice of dress (a cream, linen suit) and could only sit and cringe, imaging the sweat patches that would be there by the end of the evening.

But apart from that, the service was fairly straightforward – quite moving, in fact. I'm sure at one point I felt a tear form in my eye, but I blinked it away. Ollie looked like he was welling up too, soppy sod.

Afterwards, the plan was to make our way to the social club for the reception, following Mum and Sweaty Keith on their motorcycle and side-car. I had thought that we would be going with Rene again, but Ollie grabbed my arm and asked if we could get a separate taxi.

"There's something I need to tell you," he said.

So, I was thinking, *Uh-oh, here we go again. He's telling me that he's off again.*

Ollie waited until we were sitting in the cab and then he turned to me. "There's something else I haven't told you. I was just waiting until everything had been confirmed and now it has."

"What has?"

"Stuff from work."

I suddenly twigged. "Has this got something to do with that letter you got yesterday?"

Ollie nodded. "Yes, the letter has everything to do with it. You see that letter tells me that everything is okay, that I can move on."

"Ollie? What are you going on about?"

Ollie was biting his lip; he looked at me hard for a few seconds before continuing.

"There was an incident at work. There was a guy that I worked with, that was very good friends with Lottie. He found out about what I did to her, the affair – and he leaked it around the office."

"Bloody hell, that's awful."

Ollie shook his head, sadly. "It's what those places can be like – teasing, banter, ripping you apart. The trouble is they took it too far. One of my managers found out and he's a nasty piece of work at the best of times. He kept on and on at me. One day, he pinned me in the corner and shouted that I was a 'worthless homo' in front of the entire team. So I lost it and punched him. I broke his nose."

"Oh God!" I couldn't think of what to say. "So they sacked you?"

Ollie smiled. "Not exactly. You see this guy was not as popular as he liked to think – a few in the office were prepared to back me up and say that he made a homophobic comment. I was provoked. Sacking me might have been messy, so after an investigation the company have decided to give me a compromise agreement."

"Compromise agreement?"

"It's basically a pay-off, so that I don't take them to a tribunal and drag them through the courts. They give me a nice reference and some cash. And quite a lot of it too. And do you know what I'm going to do with it?"

"No"

"Jet off to Thailand for a few months, get some sunshine on my face. Chill out."

"Oh."

I couldn't hide my disappointment, even though I kind of knew it was coming.

"And do you know what else I want to do?" he added.

"No," I said weakly. Not really sure if I was caring anymore.

"I want to take you with me."

I was struck dumb. I just smiled at Ollie inanely.

"Really? You'd do that?"

He squeezed my shoulder. "I would *love* to. Nobody deserves it more."

The rest of the wedding passed in a blur after that. I watched the dancing, ate the food, kissed the drunken relatives, cuddled my Mum, but above everything else I was thinking – my god – I could be taken away from all of this.

I didn't even flinch when Dad arrived, boozed up with Debs on his arm, and started showing off by doing jive moves (badly) in the centre of the dance floor.

On the way home I kissed Ollie and said that I would love to come with him, as long as Dad was happy because I could never leave him if he wasn't. I told Ollie that I would have to speak to him first. I think he understood.

I then went to up to bed and checked my phone to find a text from Dan, sent much earlier in the day.

*Hi Maz. Spoke to Neil and the job's yours if you want it. P.S I've split up with Sadie xxx*

Why the hell does everything happen at once?

## Comments

**007:** So much choice. What are you going to do?

**MaisyM:** I want to go with Ollie, I'd love to see Thailand and spend time with my brother.

But I need to be with my Dad and I need the job. Would Dan understand?

**Popsicle:** And now Dan is single...I think he's interested in you!!

**MaisyM:** I'm sure he's not

**007:** I think he likes you more than you think

## Monday 19th December

### Making Plans for Maisy...

Today I told everyone that I would be leaving. It seemed a bit dramatic when I am only going for a month or so, but when you have barely taken a step outside South London, you can't stop the excitement bubbling over.

First of all, I had to tell Dad.

We were sat watching TV together, Ollie was out, so the moment felt right.

"Dad, Ollie has offered to take me on holiday with him, after Christmas," I said quickly.

He looked up, saying nothing.

"He's thinking of Thailand, but we may travel over to Malaysia. It'll be for several weeks, maybe even months..."

"Oh. Right. And how is he paying for this then?"

"He got some money from work. He thinks it would be good for us to get to know each other better... And I think he's right."

I didn't tell Dad the details of Ollie's work incident as I wasn't sure how much Ollie wanted Dad to know.

Dad sighed and then nodded slowly. "You have to go, Maisy. It'll be a chance of a lifetime."

"But what about you? Will you be okay?"

"Well...It's not forever is it? And I've got Dave for company." He eyed the dog suspiciously. "Although if he starts crapping everywhere again he might find himself out on his arse."

"He has been much better..."

"Just make sure I've got plenty of tins in the cupboard and I'll be fine. I probably won't even notice you're gone."

I couldn't help but notice a glimmer of tears in his eyes though.

A little later today, I called Dan to give him the news.

"I'm so sorry to mess you around," I said. "But this is a fantastic chance for me to get away for a bit. I hate to turn down the job, but I understand you can't keep it open for me."

There was a long pause and then Dan said, "How long will you be gone?"

"I'm not sure yet, we just want to play it by ear. Probably just a month or so."

"OK," his voice was soft. "I'll have to explain to Neil. He'll be disappointed. He really liked you."

"Really?"

"Yes, really. He said you had character and a certain charm. He thought clients would warm to you. Neil has a knack of getting it right."

"It's a shame," I admitted. "And I do hate turning down a job, especially in these times. I don't even want to ask about salary."

"Seventeen thousand to start, plus commission..."

"Oh no, Dan. Stop it." I felt like crying. "I just don't know what to do. My head says one thing and my heart says another. I just know that chances like that never usually come along. I barely know my brother and I want to. I've never been abroad and I want to. Is that so bad of me?"

"No," he said firmly. "Not at all. You go. Have an amazing time. Leave Neil to me, I'm sure we can wait a few more weeks."

"Do you think?"

"Well, maybe we could just get a temp in," he laughed. "I should be talking to Neil in the next few days. I'll let you know what he says."

"Thank you," I whispered.

"And, I wanted to tell you how bad I felt about our night out...you know, when Sadie called and, well we nearly..."

"Yeah, I know. It's okay. Are you and Sadie definitely over?"

"Definitely – I couldn't stand being with her another second. It wasn't working."

"Why?"

"Because I kept comparing her to you."

*I honestly think the stomach inside me just flipped over. I felt unable to answer, my tongue was swollen inside my mouth.*

"I'll miss you, Maz," he said gently.

"I'll miss you too," I said back.

And I meant it.


## Comments

**Popsicle:** Aw. I'm actually crying!!

**JesseBelle:** Pass the sick bucket the morning sickness has been triggered again ;o)

**Lucy Locket:** That really is sweet. How nice that you will have a job and a guy waiting for you when you get home!

**Glen @LondonRiotCleanup:** I'm gutted, but hey – I'm glad you're happy

**007:** Told you he liked you!

**MaisyM:** ;oD

### Wednesday 21st December 2011

### Christmas Drinks

Tonight has been spent in the Pride, having a drink with my girls. Poppy is off to Scotland tomorrow for Christmas with her grandparents.

Jess was having problems as Steve was already beginning to act like an idiot again, ignoring her calls, being evasive.

"I can see me bringing this kiddie up on my own," she admitted to us, sadly. "I'd rather him not be on the scene at all, if he's going to be flitting in and out whenever it suits him."

"You know you don't need him; he hardly brings much to the mix," I reminded her.

"You'd better hurry up and come back. You're down as my birthing partner now and my family are known for their early arrivals."

I nodded, smiling, not really sure how I felt about this. Of course I'll do it – she's my best friend. But I'm not sure how I'll be when presented with a load of blood and goo.

It was weird drinking in the Pride surrounded by its pathetic strands of tinsel and hanging baubles. This is all while I'm trying to write a list of what to take to Thailand with me. Luckily, Jess is lending most of my beachwear and a few dresses. I've got so little of my own to bring. I've even had to nick Mum's bright pink suitcase.

I don't feel Christmassy at all. Usually I make an effort, but this year all I've done is pull out the crappy, artificial tree from the loft and drape some aging decorations on it.

"That bloody thing's had it," my Dad complained. "It looks like it's been dug out of a skip."

"If you care so much, buy a new one," I told him, before flouncing off to get some cheap sun-cream in town.

And I've ended up in my local, crossing off what I need to take on my list, ignoring the fact that I still haven't wrapped half the presents I've got, or even brought the Christmas dinner (I'm going shopping with Ollie tomorrow). Christmas has taken a back seat.

"You might meet a hunky man out there," Poppy gushed. "Although you don't need one when you have Dan waiting here for you."

"Oh God, don't bother with blokes. Just concentrate on your tan and reading your books," Jess advised, pulling a face at Poppy.

I didn't tell them that I planned to read Mum's diary while I was away. It was all packed and ready to go. I'm not sure whether I'm looking forward to reading it or not. I think I'm a bit nervous, but I'm also intrigued, wondering if some of my questions about her will be answered.

At the end of the evening, Poppy gave me a big kiss and then handed me a small box that she had been hiding in her handbag.

"It's from both of us."

Slowly I opened it up and inside was a beautiful heart-shaped necklace.

"It's so you can remember us while you are away," Jess explained. "We really do love you."

I walked down the street that was lit up by fairy lights. I could hear a band playing Christmas anthems in the distance. A drunk man was dancing aimlessly along to the music by the side of the road, his laughter was so infectious I found myself grinning with him.

Everything was feeling quite magical. Almost new.

I couldn't help it, but I started to cry.


*Comments*

**Popsicle:** Don't forget to pack the necklace!!

**MaisyM:** I won't. I love you girls too. Will miss you loads too xx

**Thursday 22nd December 2011**

## More Goodbyes

I felt sad today, going into Pound4Pound knowing that I wouldn't be coming back, at least not as an employee. Don't get me wrong, it was far from an ideal job, but I liked the people (apart from Jed) and I liked being busy. And above all, I liked being liked.

They got me a lovely card and everyone signed it. Leon offered to take me out for drinks, but I declined. I still have presents to wrap and bits to do around the house. Also, Dad hinted that he wanted to watch some old comedy classics on TV tonight and that suited me just fine.

Then Mum called me after work. She was very emotional.

"I'm scared you won't come home, Maz," she sobbed. "I had a dream where you went abroad and stayed there. Both of you. I lost both of you. I saw it as some kind of punishment."

"I'm not staying out there. I'm hoping to have a job to come back to for a start. It's just an extended holiday."

I feel guilty that I'm going away when Mum and Sweaty Keith are having to save up for their honeymoon. They are hoping for a week in Bognor.

"Oh, I hope you are right. My dreams have never let me down before."

"Well that's rubbish for a start. You once dreamt that you were Cheryl Cole and your kneecaps kept falling off."

"Yes…well, there was that one."

"And the one when Dad ran for Mayor of London?"

"Yes, okay Maisy, you've made your point. Just promise me you'll be home soon?"

"I promise."

Honestly, anyone would think I was going away for years, not weeks.


*Comments*

**Lucy Locket:** Lol – your Mum is so funny x

**Sunday 25th December 2011**

**It's Christmas!!!**

Ollie burst into my room this morning, screaming: "It's Christmas! Has Santa been?"

I was still half asleep, having been up most of the night peeling bloody vegetables. (Why is it you have to put stupid, little crosses at the bottom of brussel sprouts? It's such a faff?)

"What are you going on about?" I muttered, pulling the duvet back over my head.

"This!"

A heavy thud landed on my bed. I peered over the top of the cover, to find a red fluffy stocking lying across me. I actually stopped believing in Father Christmas when I was five and my Dad stumbled in drunk, tripped over my dolly, screamed "JESUS!" at the top of his voice and dropped my stocking on my head.

"Aw, Ollie you shouldn't have," I said.

"It wasn't me," he protested. "It was Mr Christmas."

Inside my stocking were loads of fantastic goodies, including shower gel, body cream, sunglasses, lipstick and a beautiful notebook. Right at the bottom, stuffed into the toe were a handful of nuts and a Satsuma.

"Do you remember what Nanna used to say?" Ollie asked, as he watched me pull it all out.

I was laughing. "Of course I do!" I put on her voice. *"When I was a girl, all I got for Christmas was a Satsuma, a ha'penny and a handful of nuts and I'd be grateful..."*

Christmas Day itself was lovely. Dad was extremely chilled – he loved the beer that I brought him and was even happier with the vintage ale from Ollie. Ollie also go him some clothes, including a selection of tops.

"You trying to tart me up, son?" Dad complained. But he still pulled on one of the jumpers and seemed quite happy in it.

Dad brought me some hand cream and Ollie a book, obviously randomly picked as it was horror, not exactly Ollie's cup of tea, but at least he tried.

My dinner was average. I certainly don't think Gordon Ramsey should be concerned. I still don't know how I managed to create such lumpy gravy, but Ollie and Dad bravely ate it. They needed it as the turkey was a bit dry. I was so worried about undercooking it, I overcooked it by an hour and to be honest I've seen more juice in a Jacob's cracker. At least my carefully prepared vegetables were nice.

Dad sloped off to the pub soon after dinner, leaving us with the washing up.

"I can't do it love – delicate skin condition…"

After clearing up, me and Ollie decided to walk over to Mum's. We knew it would be the last time we'd see them before going away. We also knew that Nanna was spending the day there, which was an added bonus.

Our afternoon was spent playing Scrabble with Mum and Nanna. Sweaty Keith refused to play, claiming that board games 'gave him indigestion' (more likely he only knows about twenty legal words).

Nanna on the other hand loves board games, but she loves them too much. In fact, I would go as far as to say that she is competitive. When Ollie ended up beating her, Nanna jumped up in rage and threw her rack across the room, nearly hitting Sweaty Keith with a letter K.

"It's a stupid, bloody game anyway!" she yelled. "How the hell can qadi be a word? Who has ever uttered that word in a sentence? Who? I'd love to meet them, because I'd guarantee that they'd be a complete and utter KNOB!"

Ollie had to promise to buy her a Scrabble dictionary for her birthday to calm her down. I think she will be revising heavily for the next game.

Mum quickly packed away the game and put on the music channel instead, treating us to endless  Christmas hits, with Mum and Sweaty Keith playing 'guess the year' between them.

Nanna ended up falling asleep on the sofa, mouth open, with a box of chocolate Brazils nestled in her arm. We contemplated throwing rolled Quality Street wrappers into her gaping gob, but resisted. Okay, I lied – we did it twice, but missed.

"Will you come back here after Thailand?" I asked Ollie, as we sat together on the sofa, watching the evening unfold around us.

"I think I just might," Ollie replied softly. "I think that I have more to come back for than I realised."


**Comments**

**Lucy Locket:** Happy Christmas!!

**Glen@LondonRiotCleanup:** Happy Christmas!!! Hope 2012 is a good one for you

**Popsicle:** Happy Christmas to my best mate

**JesseBelle:** Happy Christmas hun – what a year!!

**Superstar2:** Happy Xmas xxxxxx

**007:** Happy Christmas Maisy.

I think 2012 will be great

**MaisyM:** Happy Christmas everyone!!!!!!!!


**Monday 26th December 2011**

**Up, Up and Away**

So this is my last post for a bit. Not sure how long I will be gone. I only have so many pairs of knickers, but Ollie has promised me we will go shopping at Gatwick for some more bits.

I don't like goodbyes and neither does Dad. I've just made sure that the cupboard is stacked full of beans, soup and dog food (hopefully not to be mixed up) and I have asked Debs and Norm to keep an eye on him. Even Nanna said she might pop over, and she can't stand him.

"Just don't be catching any tropical diseases," was Dad's helpful advice. "And make sure you're back for my birthday." (This is in May, so I think it's likely.)

But probably even more exciting was the text I received from Dan just minutes ago:

*I finally heard from Neil, he says he's happy to wait and so am I. Hoping to see you soon. Will miss you Dan/ 007 xx*

So Dan was my 007 all the time. He has been reading my blog since we first met. I'm not sure how I feel about that. A bit embarrassed I think.

And I'm not sure what he means by he'll be happy to wait too. Does he just mean working with me? Or maybe more? To be honest, I can't think about that at the moment – but I have to say I am a little excited by the thought. I think I might have to have a chat with him when I get back. And I can't believe I might have a job when I come home. Tanned and in employment, all I need is my own place and I might actually start to feel like a grown-up.

211

I have to go now. Ollie is shouting, saying that the taxi will be here any second. I have everything I need, including Mum's diary to read on the beach. (I've leafed through it and there's quite a lot of sex in it, the saucy mare!)

So I guess that this is goodbye for now. I hope to log on again soon. Just as long as I'm not involved in a horrific plane crash or earthquake or a pile up on the M23. Or, knowing my luck, I'll die from eating a dodgy prawn or something.

This is Maisy Malone, blogging off. Thank you for listening. I hope you will be back, just as long as I make it back alive!

xxx

14203006R00118

Printed in Great Britain
by Amazon.co.uk, Ltd.,
Marston Gate.